175
High-Impact
Cover Letters

175
HIGH-IMPACT
COVER LETTERS

SECOND EDITION

Richard H. Beatty

John Wiley & Sons, Inc.

New York • Chichester • Brisbane • Toronto • Singapore

Library of Congress Cataloging-in-Publication Data:

Beatty, Richard H., 1993–
        175 high-impact cover letters / Richard Beatty. — 2nd ed.
            p.   cm.
        Includes index.
        ISBN 0-471-12385-4 (pbk. : alk. paper)
        1. Cover letters.   2. Job hunting.   I. Title.
        HF5383.B323   1996
        808′.066651—dc20   95-52821

Printed in the United States of America
10 9 8 7 6 5 4 3 2 1

To the thousands of job applicants
who have sent me their cover letters over
the years, and whose letters have been used as the
basis for the sample letters contained in this book
Thank you!

Preface

One of the most difficult chores of running a successful job-hunting campaign is writing effective cover letters. Unlike a resume, which a job seeker can spend hours perfecting, a cover letter must often be written "on the run" but still needs to be tailored to specific circumstances. For most people, this is not an easy task. Unfortunately, in many cases, a hurriedly prepared cover letter can lead to disastrous results!

The cover letter is far too important a document to be left to chance or to be written hurriedly at the last minute. Instead, the job seeker needs to be equipped ahead of time with an arsenal of highly effective, professional cover letter models that, with only minor modification, can be rapidly deployed as needed.

This book provides the job seeker with just such an arsenal! It contains 175 highly effective cover letter samples. With slight modification, they can be utilized by the job seeker throughout the job-hunting campaign. The sample letters have been designed to meet the wide range of circumstances that the job seeker will likely encounter and to equip him or her with the ability to quickly respond with a well-written, professional document that will create a favorable impression with employers and serve to enhance his or her employment candidacy.

The reader is furnished with specific instructions and numerous models to assist in the preparation of six different types of letters: (1) the employer broadcast letter, (2) the search firm broadcast letter, (3) the advertising response letter, (4) the networking cover letter, (5) the increasingly popular resume letter, and (6) a thank-you letter. A full chapter, along with 30 or more model letters, has been dedicated to each of the six letter types.

Chapter 4, on advertising response letters, should prove particularly interesting and helpful. This chapter contains some 30 sample cover letters alongside the sample advertisements that they were designed to answer. By comparing each sample cover letter to the corresponding advertisement, readers can quickly see how to construct an efficient, high-impact letter that is tailored to the employer's specific requirements.

Also provided is a chapter on the popular resume letter, which is a cross between the cover letter and the resume. Increasingly, the resume letter is being used by the modern job seeker as a replacement for the resume. A well-designed resume letter is easy to read, creates interest in one's employment candidacy without forcing the employer to read the resume itself, and can prove to be a highly effective job-search tool.

Chapter 7 is new in this edition. Its topic is thank-you letters, an important aspect of employment letter writing. Although technically not a cover letter, a well-written thank-you letter, sent to the interviewer as a follow-up contact, can have a positive impact and offers another excellent opportunity to market your value and abilities.

With its step-by-step instructions and 175 cover letter samples, this book should greatly simplify the chore of cover letter writing for most job seekers. It gives readers all of the ammunition necessary to write highly effective, professional cover letters that will substantially enhance the overall effectiveness of their job-hunting campaign.

Best wishes for a successful job search and a rewarding career!

RICHARD H. BEATTY

West Chester, Pennsylvania
February 1996

Contents

175
High-Impact
Cover Letters

1

Importance of Cover Letters

The cover letter, which accompanies your employment resume, can clearly be a most critical tool to the overall effectiveness of your job search. If carefully thought out and well designed, it can be analogous to a good book-cover design—attracting attention, raising curiosity, compelling interest, and begging the reader to read on.

If well designed, well written, and informative, your cover letter can do much to grab the reader's attention, raise curiosity, and greatly stimulate interest in your employment candidacy. In fact, if exceptionally well written, the cover letter can sometimes stimulate sufficient interest in your credentials to convince the recipient that you are a highly desirable candidate worthy of an employment interview—without even bothering to read the resume that accompanies it.

By contrast, a poorly written cover letter can be absolutely disastrous to an otherwise successful job-hunting campaign. The way your letter is organized, what it says, how it is stated, what is included/excluded, what is highlighted/emphasized—all are critical factors for effectiveness. Cover letters that are poorly conceived and fail to give due consideration to these important factors can (and will) be fatal to your employment candidacy. The reader will discard your resume with no further thought given to your candidacy.

As an employment professional with years of experience, I have never ceased to be amazed that some people will put hours (or even days) into the preparation and design of the "perfect" resume—one that impressively highlights their qualifications and skillfully markets their credentials—and then put only five minutes' preparation time into a cover letter that causes them to "fall flat on their face." Such behavior simply defies all logic and rules of basic common sense.

Let's face it; the cover letter is the first thing that meets the reader's eye. And we have all heard and read a great deal about the importance of "first impressions" in the employment and interview process. The cover letter is no exception! It is the document that creates that all-important "first impression," and it will have a great deal of impact on how the reader "perceives" you right from the start.

If the cover letter is neat and well written, it will create a positive impression and suggest that you are someone who is neat and careful about your work. By contrast, a sloppy or poorly written cover letter will suggest that you are someone who has little concern for the quality of your work.

Besides cover letter appearance, what you say in the cover letter (and how you say it) can have considerable impact on the reader. These factors immediately tell the reader something about your general communication skills. For example, they can telegraph to the reader whether you are expressive, concise, articulate—or whether you are inexpressive, overly detailed, inarticulate, or worse. These factors (that is, what you say and how you say it) can also telegraph to the reader something about your intellectual capacity and how you think. For example, these factors can suggest to the reader that you are someone who is conceptual, strategic, analytical, and logical, or (if the letter is not carefully choreographed) that you are someone whose thinking is muddled, overly simplistic, illogical, and disorganized.

Finally, if well designed, the cover letter can do a lot to "premarket" your candidacy. If, as a result of reading your cover letter, for example, the reader is feeling positive and impressed with what you have to say, these feelings will likely spill over into the resume, which will then be read with a far less critical eye. Conversely, if the cover letter is poorly designed, your resume may not be read at all.

Although it is difficult for me to believe as an employment professional, I have had prominent people tell me that they place more stock in the cover letter than they do in the resume. Some have told me that they have invited certain candidates in for employment interviews based solely on the strength of their cover letters, without regard to the resumes. Amazingly, some of these same individuals have even volunteered that they seldom bother to read the resume if the cover letter is impressive.

So, considering the overwhelming evidence, one doesn't have to be a rocket scientist to come to the conclusion that the cover letter is a very important document indeed. How it is designed and written can make a significant difference in one's job-hunting success. Your cover letter clearly deserves your deliberate and careful attention if you are serious about maximizing your opportunities in the marketplace. This book, if carefully followed, should provide you with a distinct competitive advantage.

TYPES OF COVER LETTERS

When most people think about cover letters, they have in mind the letter that is used to introduce their resume to a prospective employer. Actually, there are five types of cover letters, each designed a little differently and each having a slightly different purpose:

1. Letters to Employers.
2. Letters to Search Firms.
3. Advertising Response Letters.
4. Networking Cover Letters.
5. Resume Letters.

This book will thoroughly familiarize you with each of these letter types and provide you with numerous examples as the basis for modeling and writing your own effective cover letters. By carefully studying these sample letters, along with the instructions at the beginning of each chapter, you should have all you need to write a highly effective cover letter and to add a good deal of zest and positive impact to your job-hunting campaign.

2

Letters to Employers

If you are contemplating use of a mass-mailing program to send your resume to employers, you need to know that you are playing a "numbers game." Although a standard element of most well-planned job-hunting campaigns, direct mailings have not been known for producing significant results when compared to the use of such job-hunting sources as networking, recruitment advertising, and employment agencies. Nonetheless, should you elect to use the direct-mail approach, you will need an effective cover letter to help you realize a reasonable return on the time you invest in this process.

Professionals who specialize in the direct-mail business have long known that, if well executed, a direct-mail campaign will generally produce a return in the 3 to 5 percent range. Thus, a targeted mailing of 300 letters should be expected to generate only 9 to 15 responses. If you are planning to utilize this approach as part of your job search program, your mailing should perhaps target several hundred firms.

In a tight labor market, characterized by high unemployment and a glut of available candidates, the direct-mail approach can be even less effective. Recent research has shown a positive response rate of only 3 percent during such a market. Some employment experts feel that the rate of return is likely to be even lower, depending on the severity of employment market conditions.

When considering whether to utilize direct mail as part of your job-hunting program, the important thing to remember is that it takes only a *single* favorable response to generate a job interview. If it's the right job, this approach can pay off rather handsomely, providing you with an exciting and rewarding career opportunity.

So don't be discouraged by the meager statistical results cited here. Instead, make the direct-mail campaign a component of your job search plan. Just remember to maintain realistic expectations.

THE BROADCAST LETTER

In the parlance of employment professionals, the cover letter used by job seekers to transmit their resumes to prospective employers is commonly known as a *broadcast* letter. This name comes from the use of the letter to broadcast the candidate's employment availability to a large audience.

The composition of the broadcast letter will be extremely important to the outcome of your direct-mail campaign. If designed and written well, it will improve your response rate and substantially increase the number of interview opportunities presented to you. Conversely, if poorly designed or poorly written, it will detract from your mailing results and reduce (or even eliminate) your opportunities for employment interviews.

If you are going to have an effective direct-mail campaign, you must spend some quality time in designing a well-written cover letter that will successfully market your skills and capabilities to prospective employers.

LIST OF TARGET COMPANIES

Wherever possible, your broadcast cover letter should be directed to a specific individual at each of the target firms you have selected. Research indicates that "personally targeted" mailings are received more favorably and are more likely to generate a favorable response. A letter simply addressed to the "Manager of Manufacturing" without the manager's name does not engender warm feelings on the part of the recipient and "just doesn't cut it" if you expect to maximize the results of your mailing campaign!

When you research your list of target companies, it is imperative that you find the name and exact title of the individual you wish to target. The rule of thumb is: Address the manager of the person for whom you would likely work. If you cannot identify that person, then direct your letter to the executive in charge of the functional area you have chosen to target.

National offices of industry or professional associations can provide excellent sources of personnel information. The association's president can frequently identify publications, either industry- or profession-specific, that provide the kind of in-depth personnel information you will need to prepare an effective mailing list.

THE CARDINAL RULE

When preparing a direct-mail program, follow this cardinal rule: Never mail your cover letter and resume to the personnel (or employment) department! These departments are normally inundated with unsolicited resumes and often are not staffed or equipped to efficiently handle the volume of employment mail received. During recent years, corporate downsizing has particularly affected personnel departments through drastic cuts in their resources.

Additionally, it is important to realize that the personnel (or employment) department is frequently aware only of the organization's "formal" openings.

That is, they know only about those employment openings that have been formally approved by management for hiring purposes. By contrast, they may be totally unaware of "informal" or "hidden" employment openings—those that are in the minds of their client managers and have not yet been formally communicated.

This phenomenon of informal employment openings has been dubbed the "hidden job market" by the professional employment community. Estimates by employment professionals suggest that the size of this hidden job market is as much as 70 to 80 percent of the entire job market. It is also said that these hidden jobs are most often filled long before they have a chance to become known to the general public through recruitment advertising, employment agencies, and search firms.

Targeting your mailing directly to functional managers, rather than to the personnel (or employment) department, gives you the opportunity to access this hidden job market. Receipt of your broadcast cover letter, along with your resume, could be just the trigger mechanism to generate an interview rather than a standard "no interest" form letter from the firm's personnel department.

You can see now why it is so important to target your letters to specific managers if you wish to maximize the results of your direct-mail program.

THE VALUE-ADDED CONCEPT

When designing your general broadcast cover letter, it is imperative to bear in mind that employers don't fill positions just for the sake of filling them. They are looking for candidates who are capable of accomplishing specific results—persons who can "add value" to their organizations.

Some careful analysis of the duties of your targeted position (job search objective) should yield some good clues as to the results and value employers expect of a successful candidate. Good cover letter design will serve to highlight your ability to contribute specific results and add value in these important areas. The following exercise should help you to define these areas:

1. What are the key, ongoing, functional accountabilities of the position for which you are applying?
2. In each of these key functional areas, what are the end results likely to be desired by the employer?
3. What important results have you achieved in each of these key areas that would be of interest to the employer and could serve to communicate your "value" to the employer?

If you are just entering the job market for the first time, you will need a slightly different approach. You will want to focus on specific skills and attributes you possess that should enable you to perform the job particularly well. The following questions may help you to organize your thoughts on this matter.

1. What key problems will you need to solve if you are to be successful in performing your targeted job?

2. What key knowledge and/or skills will be required in order for you to solve these problems and achieve successful job performance?

3. Which of these qualifications (knowledge/skills) do you possess?

4. What evidence of your ability can you cite to apply these qualities?

5. What personal attributes are considered important in successfully performing your targeted job?

6. Which of these attributes do you possess?

7. What evidence can you cite regarding these attributes?

The sample cover letters contained in this chapter will effectively illustrate how these key accomplishments and important personal traits can be highlighted to your advantage.

KEY ELEMENTS OF BROADCAST LETTER

Review of the sample cover letters provided in this chapter will reveal that there are five key elements to effective broadcast cover letter composition:

1. An introductory paragraph that includes a statement of your job search objective.

2. A brief summary paragraph that summarizes your overall background and experience.

3. A "selling" (value-adding) paragraph that highlights specific results achieved by you in those areas known to be important to successful job performance.

4. A request for action on your candidacy.

5. A statement of appreciation for the employer's consideration of your employment candidacy.

Notice these key elements in the following cover letter samples, which have been provided as models for your own effective direct-mail cover letters.

501 Lexington Avenue
Lansing, MI 47397

January 29, 1998

Mr. Norman D. Crawford
Director of Marketing
Cracker Barrel Foods
150 Interplex Drive
Superior, WI 54751

Dear Mr. Crawford:

I am writing to present my credentials for the position of Brand Manager, a position for which I am exceptionally well-qualified. I am confident that you will quickly realize my ability to make major contributions to Cracker Barrel Foods' marketing efforts upon reviewing the enclosed resume.

As my resume will attest, I have established an excellent reputation for pumping new life into old brands and making them perform. Examples of my accomplishments in this area are:

Doubled frozen pizza market share in only nine months

Increased microwave popcorn market share by 99% in two years

Improved direct mail orders of premium crackers by 38% in 18 months through use of creative coupons

My contributions to new brands have been equally noteworthy. For example:

Achieved 29% market share penetration for line of low salt shredded cheeses within one year of market introduction

Completed national roll-out of "Kids Packs," a line of single-serving, fruit-flavored yogurt cups, in six months, reaching 18% market penetration

Perhaps I can make similar contributions to Cracker Barrel Foods in the marketing of either new or existing brands.

Should you have room in your organization for a top-notch marketing professional who is capable of making immediate contributions to your marketing efforts and adding some real profit to your bottom line, please give me a call. I look forward to hearing from you.

Thank you for your consideration.

Sincerely,

Curtis M. Mitchell

Curtis M. Mitchell

CMM/rac

Enclosure

122 Graduate Tower, East
Drake University
Des Moines, IA 50311

February 10, 1998

Ms. Sandra A. Covington
Director of Marketing and Sales
Hoffman Industries
600 West Main Street
Cleveland, OH 66306

Dear Ms. Covington:

I am very interested in talking with you about employment as a Sales Representative Trainee with Hoffman Industries, and hope you will give my candidacy strong consideration. I feel I have the necessary skills and interest to be an excellent contributor to your organization, and would like the opportunity to demonstrate this through a personal interview with your recruiter during Hoffman's forthcoming recruiting schedule at Drake University. My resume is enclosed for your reference.

Although short on experience, Ms. Covington, I am long on effort and enthusiasm. I am an outgoing, friendly individual who would enjoy building strong interpersonal relationships with valued customers. My strong service orientation and bias for action would serve your company well in responding to the needs and concerns of your clients. My drive, determination and leadership abilities are well-evidenced by the following accomplishments:

- Grade Point Average of 3.7/4.0

- Fraternity President, Senior Year
  Fraternity Vice President, Junior Year
  Pledge Chairman, Sophomore Year

- Captain, Varsity Crew Team, Senior Year
  Member, Varsity Crew Team, 3 Years
  Co-Captain, Varsity Swim Team, Junior Year
  Member, Varsity Swim Team, 4 Years

I would like the chance to put my energy, drive and enthusiasm to work for a company such as yours. May I have the opportunity to further discuss your requirements during a personal meeting with your representative on February 22nd?

Sincerely,

Mark D. Wainwright

Mark D. Wainwright

MDW/ael

Enclosure

PHYLLIS C. RADCLIFFE
27 Darlington Woods Estates
Bloomington, MN 55437

May 18, 1998

Mr. James J. Blau
President and COO
Igloo Products, Inc.
300 Sheridan Avenue
Northbrook, IL 60062

Dear Mr. Blau:

As the Chief Operating Officer of a leading company in the plastics industry, I am sure that you are well aware of the value of a top-notch manufacturing executive to a profit-oriented corporation. If you are currently seeking a proven contributor to lead your manufacturing operations, I encourage you to give serious consideration to my credentials.

As a manufacturing executive with an M.S. degree in Engineering and over 15 years of solid achievement and career progression, I have established a distinguished reputation as a strong profit contributor. Among some of my more notable accomplishments are:

- a 36% reduction in manufacturing costs in a major furnace operation (annual savings of $13 million)

- on-time and below cost start-up of a $435 million tube manufacturing plant (project savings of $7 million)

- a 28% reduction in labor costs over a three-plant operation through an extensive work redesign project (annual savings of $5.9 million)

- a 68% reduction in scrap and 86% reduction in customer complaints through implementation of an SPC-based total quality effort (annual savings of $4.8 million)

Perhaps we should meet to discuss the contributions that I could make to your firm if employed as a senior member of your manufacturing team. Should you agree, I can be reached during office hours at (612) 737-2310 or at (612) 555-6731 in the evening.

Sincerely,

Phyllis C. Radcliffe

Phyllis C. Radcliffe

PCR/rms

Enclosure

1336 Dutton Circle
Collingswood, NJ 08108

October 26, 1999

Dr. Lance D. Spellman
Vice President Research & Development
Lilly Industries, Inc.
2300 Parklake Drive, NE
Atlanta, GA 30345

Dear Dr. Spellman:

Lilly Industries, Inc., as one of the leaders in the field of polymer chemistry, might be interested in a seasoned Product Development Chemist with a demonstrated record of achievement as a new product innovator. My credentials include an M.S. in Polymer Chemistry with over 15 years research experience in the polymer industry.

As you can see from the enclosed resume, my reputation as a creative, innovative contributor is well supported by some 22 registered patents and an additional 18 patent disclosures. My work has led to the successful introduction of 12 new products which now account for over $250 million in annual sales revenues.

I have extensive experience in the following specialty areas:

> Organic and Polymer Specialty Chemicals:
> - Water Treatment Chemicals
> - Oil Field and Mining Chemicals
> - Consumer Products Based on Water-Soluble Polymers
>
> Polymers, Rubbers and Plastics:
> - New Polymers and Plastics - Synthetic Approach
> - New Polymers and Plastics - Physio-Chemical Approach

My current salary is $82,000, and I have no geographical restrictions.

Should you have an appropriate opportunity available as a member of your research staff, Dr. Spellman, I would welcome the opportunity to meet with you to discuss the contributions that I might make to your new product development efforts. I can be reached during evening hours at (313) 528-9375.

Thank you for your consideration, and I look forward to hearing from you.

Sincerely yours,

Leon C. Madgzinski

Leon C. Madgzinski

LCM/mmb

Enclosure

CALVIN H. FURHMAN

135 Stockton Street
Reston, VA 22090

Office: (703) 492-2967
Home: (703) 676-3304

April 21, 1998

Ms. Anne B. Morris
Engineering Manager
Gilbert Paper Company
2515 McKinney Avenue
Menasha, WI 54952

Dear Ms. Morris:

I am interested in a position as a Project Engineer with Gilbert Paper Company. Review of my resume will reveal that I have strong project experience with P.H. Glatfelter Company, one of your key competitors.

I graduated with a B.S. degree in Mechanical Engineering from Princeton University, and have six years of paper machine project experience. I enjoy an excellent reputation for bringing projects in on time and at or below budget. Some key project experience includes:

- Completion of a $54 million twin wire, forming section rebuild project on-time and under budget ($1.2 million savings)

- Lead wet end Project Engineer for purchase, design and installation of a new $150 million Beloit paper machine ($120,000 savings)

- Engineered, installed and started-up $45 million rebuild of after dryer section of twin wire tissue machine (project completed two months ahead of schedule with savings of $1/2 million)

Although well-versed in most machine configurations, I am especially knowledgeable of twin wire formers and some of the newer, state-of-the-art sheet forming technology. These qualifications could prove very additive to those companies interested in upgrading their overall papermaking technology.

If you are currently seeking a strong paper machine project engineer, I would appreciate the opportunity to further discuss my qualifications with you. Thank you for your consideration.

Sincerely yours,

Calvin H. Furhman

CHF/mbs

Enclosure

DONNA J. BYRNES
214 Blair Mill Road
Anaheim, CA 92805
(714) 255-3085

March 15, 1997

Mr. Jeffrey S. Sheara
Vice President of Human Resources
Intervoice, Inc.
17811 Waterview Parkway
Garland, TX 75042

Dear Mr. Sheara:

Enclosed please find my resume for the position of Director of Employment. Should you have an opening at this level, I am confident that you will find my qualifications intriguing.

My credentials include an M.S. in Industrial Relations from Arizona State University with 14 years of solid human resources experience. This includes nearly nine years in the employment function - six as Manager of Administrative Employment with Emmerson Electronics, Inc., and nearly three years as a National Practice Director for Russell J. Reynolds, a premiere international executive search consulting firm.

I have also managed a Fortune 200 employment function with responsibility for recruitment of executive, managerial and professional employees for a wide range of functional areas. I enjoy a strong reputation for cost-effective, timely and quality recruitment, and am thoroughly versed in state-of-the-art behavioral-based interviewing and assessment methodology.

If you seek a knowledgeable professional to manage your corporate employment function, I hope that you will give me a call so that we may discuss your requirements and the contributions that I can make to your company.

Sincerely

Donna J Byrnes

Donna J. Byrnes

DJB/jmc

Enclosure

GREGORY D. MUSICK

311 Connestoga Drive
Wichita, KS 67202
(316) 741-7255

August 19, 1998

Mr. Warren A. Davidson
Manager of Corporate Accounting
Olin Corporation
120 Long Ridge Road
P.O. Box 1355
Newark, NJ 08923

Dear Mr. Davidson:

I am writing to apply for the position of Cost Accountant in your Corporate Accounting Department. I feel that I have excellent qualifications for this position, and would appreciate your careful consideration of the enclosed resume.

A 1991 graduate of Villanova University with a B.S. in Accounting, I have over seven years of employment in the Accounting profession. This includes some four years as an Auditor with Coopers & Lybrand and another three years as a Cost Accountant with Burlington Industries. I have received excellent professional training and, throughout my career, as copies of past performance evaluations will attest, I have consistently attained the highest ratings possible.

Current annual compensation is $65,000, and I would expect a competitive increase in keeping with my qualifications and experience level.

Although open to relocation, my preference is for the mid-Atlantic region. Other locations may be of interest dependent upon the specifics of the opportunity.

If you feel that your Corporate Accounting Department could benefit from the contributions of a seasoned, knowledgeable Cost Accountant, I would appreciate hearing from you.

Thank you for your consideration, and I look forward to hearing from you.

Sincerely yours,

Gregory D. Musick

Gregory D. Musick

Enclosure

ARLENE P. SHAPIRO
926 Cardinal Avenue
Houston, Texas 77070
(713) 334-7933

May 24, 1998

Mr. Robert J. Ellis
Chief Financial Officer
Drake Industries
750 Parkway Drive, South
Wayne, NJ 07763

Dear Mr. Ellis:

If you are currently in the market for an accomplished Senior Financial Analyst who has established an excellent reputation for successful acquisition analysis, the enclosed resume should prove interesting to you.

My credentials include an M.B.A. in Finance from the University of Georgia and over six years acquisition analysis with the Business Development Department of a Fortune 100 food company. During this period, I completed analysis of 28 acquisition candidates, which resulted in the acquisition of six highly profitable companies. These included:

  - a $40 million acquisition of a baking company that has achieved an
    average ROI of 18% for the first three years of ownership

  - a $28 million acquisition of a food distribution company showing a 22%
    ROI in the 3rd year of operation

  - a $62 million purchase of a food wrap company that yielded a 12% return
    during first year following acquisition

Importantly, all acquisitions have proven highly profitable, with the poorest performer achieving an ROI of 8.2%. Additionally, all acquisitions were completed at a very attractive price-to-net-profit ratio.

Mr. Ellis, I would welcome the opportunity to meet with you personally to discuss the kinds of contributions I might make to Drake Industries as a member of its Business Development staff. If you see this as a worthwhile investment, I can be reached on a confidential basis at (713) 877-9075 during business hours, or at my home phone, above, during the evening.

Very truly yours,

Arlene P. Shapiro

Arlene P. Shapiro

Enclosure

BYRON D. EVANS

1432 Church Lane
Birmingham, AL 35202

Home: (205) 413-8996
Office: (205) 227-9040

October 16, 1998

Ms. Josephine M. Durkin
Senior Vice President - Administration
Pneumatic Tool Company
1901 Diplomat Drive
Springfield, MO 20355

Dear Ms. Durkin:

As the senior administrative executive for Pneumatic Tool Company, perhaps you are in need of a talented Purchasing Manager who can almost certainly make immediate contributions to the bottom line of your company.

A Senior Purchasing Agent for a Fortune 200, $2.8 billion consumer products company, I have enjoyed a reputation as a "tough but fair negotiator", who has made significant cost savings contributions to my employer. These have included:

- consolidated corporate-wide packaging supplies purchases with
  resultant annual savings of $35 million

- contributed $12 million annual savings through conversion from
  oil to biomass fuels with long-term purchase contract

- saved $8 million annually in inventory costs through installation
  of computerized raw materials tracking and forecasting system

- successfully negotiated five-year knock-down carton contract with
  major supplier worth $5.5 million savings annually

Educational credentials include a B.S. in Packaging from Michigan State University and an M.B.A. in Finance from Penn State University. I have more than 15 years purchasing experience with a major international corporation, and have been professionally active in my field.

Compensation requirements are in the low $80,000 range, and I am open to relocation anywhere in the United States.

Should you feel my background qualifies me for a current corporate management assignment at Pneumatic Tool Company, I would welcome the opportunity to meet with you. Please contact me at my home in the evening.

I appreciate your consideration.

Sincerely,

Byron D. Evans

Byron D. Evans

2401 Hillcrest Lane
Everett, WA 98206
August 29, 1998

Mr. Preston D. Franks
Director of MIS
Brunswick Corporation
One North Field Court
Lenoir, NC 28633

Dear Mr. Franks:

As today's economy and competitive pressures place tighter constraints on business, IT professionals with a diverse background can provide greater value when budgets are tight.

As a versatile MIS professional, I have experience in project management for a wide variety of business applications in systems and database design, quality assurance, troubleshooting and programming. My B.B.A. in Accounting has given me an exceptional understanding of financial applications.

While at Condata, my hands-on management style and strong technical skills have enabled me to meet deadlines in high-pressure environments. I am seeking a position in applications management developing business systems, or a liaison position between IT and the user community.

My current compensation is $65,000. Should you have an appropriate opening which parallels my background, I would appreciate a personal interview. I look forward to hearing from you.

Thank you for considering my credentials.

Very truly yours,

Justine C. Kimmell

Justine C. Kimmell

JCK/la

Enclosure

722 Ridge Avenue
Shelton, CT 06484

Home: (203) 676-4461
Office: (203) 926-1801

April 18, 1997

Ms. Marguerite A. Guilford
Vice President of Human Resources
Combined Communications Services, Inc.
1500 North Washington Road
Yorba Linda, CA 92627

Dear Ms. Guilford:

I am currently seeking a position as Training and Development Manager for a medium-sized manufacturing company. I am a hands-on, results-oriented leader with a comprehensive background in training design, development and delivery. The enclosed resume details the specifics of my experience and accomplishments.

My background spans over ten years of diverse training and development experience, providing support to a variety of functional clients. In all cases I have been successful in getting strong client support and ownership of the programs delivered. The following highlights some of my key accomplishments:

- Directed training of 200 person field sales organization for a major electronics distribution company

- Used assessment methodology as the basis for constructing "high performance models" for certain key management jobs. Assessed key managers against these models as the basis for defining key management development needs/priorities.

- Designed and delivered company's first highly successful introductory course to total quality management -- over 500 managers trained across 3 divisions.

- Developed methodology for linking training needs with business strategy, and put in place a reliable method for providing quantitative measurement of the effectiveness of management training and development programs.

Based upon my job experience and educational qualifications, I am confident that I can bring effective leadership to your training function and improve the overall human resource effectiveness and productivity of your company. I would appreciate the opportunity to further discuss my credentials with you during a face-to-face interview.

I hope to hear from you shortly.

Yours very truly,

Maureen M. Courtland

Maureen M. Courtland

MMC/ard

Enclosure

SAMUEL P. COULTER
1180 Seminole Trail
Louisville, KY 40202

November 12, 1998

Mr. Gerald Abrams
Vice President
Environmental Affairs Department
Columbia Chemical Company
1600 Parkwood Circle, SE
Atlanta, GA 30339

Dear Mr. Abrams:

I am seeking a position where I can apply my experience as an environmental specialist. As an Environmental Project Manager in the Environmental Affairs Department of the Dow Chemical Company, I have gained experience in many areas of the environmental industry, especially hazardous substance and waste management as well as environmental legislation and compliance requirements.

Specific areas of accomplishment include:

- Company compliance with applicable local, state, and federal environmental regulations nationwide.

- Design and implementation of training programs to limit company risk and liability in the hazardous substance management field.

- Research and evaluation of cost-effective methods for hazardous substance reduction, recycling and conservation.

I am interested in an industry position in environmental compliance, hazardous substance management, and/or industrial environmental training and education. I am interested in a company that has a strong interest in developing pro-active programs to limit liability and risk in environmental affairs.

My resume is enclosed. Thank you for reviewing my credentials, and I look forward to hearing from you.

Sincerely,

Samuel P. Coulter

Samuel P. Coulter

SPC/sas

Enclosure

ARNOLD D. SULLIVAN

902 Hampton Court
San Antonio, TX 78229

Home: (210) 898-3062
Office: (210) 593-7100

January 20, 1998

Mr. James R. Abernathy
Chairman of the Board
B.F. Goodrich Company
Specialty Polymers & Chemicals Division
3925 Embassy Parkway, Bldg. 6
Cleveland, OH 44141

Dear Mr. Abernathy:

I am seeking a CEO position in the chemical industry. My professional career exhibits a record of strong achievement and significant contributions. I am a top performing chemical industry executive with an extensive sales, manufacturing, research and operations background.

Throughout my career, I recruited, selected and developed very talented managers. I utilized persistence, technical expertise and interpersonal skills to establish and build long-term relationships with diverse customers. I analyzed, evaluated and led entry into new market niches enabling the company to generate significant profits, and am recognized as a creative manager with strong strategic planning, communications, listening, and operational skills. The following highlight some of my key accomplishments:

- Analyzed markets, determined special market niches, shifted product line and
  aggressively led entry into new markets resulting in sales growth of 300% and a
  sizeable profit improvement ($5 million to $13.5 million).

- Exercised operational P&L responsibility for a $30 million corporation manufacturing
  industrial specialty O.E.M. paints and coatings.

- Landed major industrial accounts (Budd/Jeep Wrangler, Clarke Equipment,
  Caterpillar Trailer, Strick, and Fruehauf) by building solid relationships through
  persistent and creative presentations, development of superior products and
  quality service.

If my qualifications are of interest, Mr. Abernathy, I would be delighted to meet with you to further explore opportunities with your fine company. I hope that we will have the opportunity to meet shortly, and I look forward to hearing from you.

Sincerely,

Arnold D. Sullivan

ADS/mas

Enclosure

GRACE M. DAVENPORT
144 Marina Boulevard
Baltimore, MD 21203

March 15, 1997

Mr. Stuart A. Hartman
Vice President MIS
Apogee Enterprises Company
123 North Wacker Drive
Chicago, IL 60606

Dear Mr. Hartman:

Enclosed is my resume outlining more than 15 years extensive experience in corporate telecommunications. In summary, my credentials include:

- broad experience in international computer networking

- design and implementation of voice, data and LAN systems

- in-depth experience with telecommunications and information processing technologies

- interpersonal skills for interfacing well with all levels of management

I would like to put this expertise to work in a senior telecommunications management and/or internal consulting position.

Although I am concentrating my search in the mid-Atlantic United States, I would consider other locations for the right opportunity.

If you are currently searching for someone with my credentials, I would be pleased to meet with you to discuss how I might help you to solve some of your more difficult telecommunications problems. Thank you for your consideration.

Sincerely,

Grace M. Davenport

Grace M. Davenport

Enclosure

GEORGE C. HAWORTH

22 Stockton Street
Ogden, UT 84401

Home: (801) 966-0246
Office: (801) 625-3500

May 20, 1998

Ms. Suzanne C. Spence
Director of Sales
Atari Computer Corporation
44 Whippany Road
Four Falls Industrial Court
Schaumburg, IL 60173

Dear Ms. Spence:

Are you looking for a salesperson for the information processing industry? Maybe I can help you. I am the corporate representative for twenty major customers at IBM Corporation. Based on this experience I can:

- Meet large global customers' total information systems requirements

- Negotiate worldwide volume purchase agreements

- Sell in international markets

- Respond to the concerns of senior management

- Leverage all corporate resources to achieve customer satisfaction

Although other factors such as career growth are of primary importance to me, you should know that my total compensation is $75,000.

I appreciate your consideration.

Very truly yours,

George C. Haworth

George C. Haworth

GCH/jos

Enclosure

608 Holly Lane
Caldwell, NJ 07006
June 22, 1997

Ms. Joan L. Garfield
Director Research & Development
Tyvec Building Products Corporation
4550 State Street
McLean, VA 22102

Dear Ms. Garfield:

I am a registered engineer in the state of New Jersey, and I am presently seeking a position in the roofing industry. A copy of my resume is enclosed, and I would like to talk with you should you have an appropriate opportunity for me at Tyvec Building Products.

My most recent assignment was to manage projects at CertainTeed to develop products for the commercial roofing industry. Part of my responsibility was to provide support to sales people, when they had questions of a technical nature from their engineering or architectural customers.

I have experience in quality assurance and the application of control charting to a large insulation line at CertainTeed. This resulted in a 23% reduction in scrap and a 76% reduction in customer complaints.

I am seeking a position as a team leader or manager in product or process development, or in quality assurance. My compensation requirements are in the $65,000 to $70,000 range, and I am open to relocation.

I would welcome the opportunity to talk with you and discuss the technical contributions I could make to Tyvec Building Products Corporation, especially in the development of exciting new roofing products.

Thank you for reviewing my credentials, and I look forward to hearing from you shortly.

Sincerely,

Grant W. Peirce

Grant W. Peirce

Enclosure

LORETTA P. GOODWIN
2246 Sunset Avenue
East Brunswick, NJ 08816

April 16, 1998

Mr. Richard J. Purcell
Director of Quality
Cascade Electronic Corporation
One Monument Square
Syracuse, NY 13221

Dear Mr. Purcell:

I am seeking a position as a Facilitator for Total Quality Management in a firm already using TQM, or one just beginning TQM implementation.

Beginning with BS and MS degrees in engineering and following with 15 years experience with Westinghouse, I have built a solid career foundation in shop operations, manufacturing engineering and plant management.

Three years ago, I became convinced of the potential of Total Quality Management and began some TQM initiatives with the Electric Motors Division. This proved highly successful, but, due to recent budget cutbacks, many of the resources targeted for further implementation of these programs have been temporarily frozen.

I am now seeking an opportunity to continue my efforts with a company that has a firm commitment to Total Quality implementation. I have much to contribute and would welcome the change.

Should you have an appropriate opening on your quality management staff, I would appreciate the opportunity to explore employment possibilities with you. Thank you for your consideration.

Sincerely,

Loretta P. Goodwin

Loretta P. Goodwin

LPG/jmc

Enclosure

562 Grammercy Lane   Home: (207) 773-6438
Portland, ME 04112   Office: (207) 834-2950

April 10, 1997

Mr. Howard T. Gross
President
Great Lakes Energy Corporation
10 West Lafayette Corporate Center
Ann Arbor, MI 48107-8600

Dear Mr. Gross:

Please take 60 seconds to consider a senior executive who has:

- Directed operations of eight international manufacturing
  companies with a combined sales volume of $120 million

- Increased profits by 40%, reduced late deliveries by 76%
  and increased market share by 15%

- As CFO, arranged debt and equity financing, implemented
  new manufacturing and accounting systems for a firm that
  grew from $18 million to $160 million in 20 months

- As a consultant, created corporate strategy for a $6
  billion company

- MBA from Harvard and BS in Engineering from Princeton

- High energy, excellent interpersonal skills and experience
  to meet challenging opportunities such as rapid growth,
  business decline and turnaround situations.

Should you have room on your senior management staff for someone
with my qualifications and experience, please contact me so that we
can meet personally. Thank you.

Sincerely,

Mark D. Donnelly

Mark G. Donnelly

MGD/fam

Enclosure

CYNTHIA G. CARRINGTON
237 Balboa Street
Indianapolis, IN 46268
(317) 293-7753

June 26, 1998

Mr. Timothy J. Bruskman
Vice President Operations
Snapple Beverage Company
4040 North Meridian Street
Horsham, PA 19044

Dear Mr. Bruskman:

I am seeking an Operations Management position at the plant, division or corporate level with a major player in the food and beverage industry. Please consider my credentials.

As my resume will show, I have had excellent progression in the field of Operations Management with one of the top U.S. consumer products companies. Pepsi-Cola, as you may know, has been ranked by *Fortune* magazine among the top six best run companies in America.

In my current position as Group Plant Manager (three plants) for Pepsi Midwest, I have been credited with annual cost savings exceeding $2 million as the result of several innovative cost reduction programs recently implemented. I have just been awarded Pesi's coveted "High Performer Award" for my contributions.

Prior assignments have been equally productive, and I have consistently demonstrated the ability to achieve superior results. I pride myself on staying current in all major new developments in the field of Operations and push hard for the implementation of those that will readily increase ease of operations and reduce operating costs.

Should you be in the market for a proven contributor as a member of your Operations Team, Mr. Bruskman, your time would be well spent in meeting with me. Much of what I have already done at Pepsi might well be transferable to Snapple Beverage, and could result in substantial savings to your company.

Should you wish to contact me, I can be reached during the day at (317) 993-3506, or at the above number during evening hours. Thank you for your consideration.

Sincerely,

Cynthia G. Carrington

Cynthia G. Carrington

CGC/pad

Enclosure

977 Green Bay Avenue
Milwaukee, WI 53201

March 12, 1997

Mr. Vincent D. Campbell
Senior Vice President
Technology Division
Niagra Telecommunications, Inc.
180 Erie Boulevard
New York, NY 10038

Dear Mr. Campbell:

Attached is my resume. I am currently seeking a Director level position in the Technical Services area. My background is predominantly Telecommunications with areas of expertise in Training, Publications, and Field Service.

If you feel that my resume warrants consideration for opportunities at Niagra Telecommunications, please contact me at (414) 816-9402 or (414) 635-9576.

Thank you for your time and consideration.

Sincerely,

Owen D Johnson

Owen D. Johnson

ODJ/jes

Attachment

BERNARD M. FOX
820 Chancellor Street
Nashville, TN 18755

May 22, 1997

Ms. Gail M. Dwyer
Director of Corporate Planning
Northrup Corporation
Electronic Systems Division
600 Hicks Road
Rolling Meadows, IL 60008

Dear Ms. Dwyer:

Do you have need for an employee who can provide management with timely information on which crucial decisions (e.g., marketing of company products, the opening of new branches, diversification of company operations, examination of the effects of new tax laws, preparation of economic forecasts, etc.) are made?

I hold an M.S. degree in Economics and Operations Research and am seeking a position with a growing organization that can fully challenge my research capabilities in pursuit of the firm's objectives.

The enclosed resume reflects solid achievement both in the classroom and during my brief professional career. Whether in the classroom or at the workplace, I have been consistently able to meet near-term objectives while developing the tools to successfully tackle future requirements.

Thank you for your time. I look forward to hearing from you. References will be furnished upon request.

Sincerely,

Bernard M. Fox

Bernard M. Fox

BMF/dcb

Enclosure

KIRK J. CAMERON

2175 Turner Lane
Columbia, MD 21046

Home: (410) 455-9776
Office: (410) 348-6052

August 31, 1998

Ms. Donna M. Barnes
Director of MIS
Powell Industries, Inc.
4 Penn Center Plaza, 10th Floor
Philadelphia, PA 19101

Dear Ms. Barnes:

I am seeking a position in data processing management and have enclosed my resume for review against your current requirements.

My background in data processing includes programming, systems analysis, project management, data base administration and MIS department management.

For the past seven years, I have been the Information Center Manager at Reliance Insurance Company in Gaithersburg, MD, responsible for planning, budgeting, organizing and managing the daily operations of this department. In addition to supporting all end user computing on the IBM 3090 mainframe and personal computers, I am responsible for evaluating PC hardware and software, establishing PC standards and policies, consulting in the design of PC applications and maintaining both mainframe and PC security controls.

I am seeking a position in the $65,000 to $70,000 range and have no relocation restrictions.

Should you have an appropriate opening in your operations, I would appreciate the opportunity to meet with you and the members of your staff to see how my qualifications might align with your requirements. Thank you for your consideration, and I look forward to hearing from you shortly.

Very truly yours,

Kirk J. Cameron

Kirk J. Cameron

KJC/amt

Enclosure

GUY M. DeMARCO
110 Demarest Drive
Jacksonville, FL 33923
(407) 476-5012

June 15, 1998

Mr. Raymnond D. Osborne
Vice President of Marketing
Hamilton Beach Corporation
1300 Cranston Street
Richmond, VA 23261

Dear Mr. Osborne:

In the course of attempting to revitalize and strengthen your
company's sales and marketing strategy, you may have a requirement
for an accomplished advertising executive.

Having been continually challenged and rapidly promoted, my career
covers a variety of products and services, including packaged
goods, insurance, technical/industrial businesses and corporate
financial/image communications. More specifically, I have:

> Developed the marketing analysis and implemented creative
> planning which led to improved sales for a mature,
> declining brand.
>
> In a similar role, helped maintain another brand's growth
> momentum with an imaginative advertising and promotion
> program for a line extension.
>
> In addition, I have strengthened and managed corporate
> advertising which helped change the ways in which senior
> business executives, consumers and the financial
> community perceived several major blue chip corporations.

While challenging marketing and customer communications problems
are of primary importance to me, you should know that my total
compensation requirements are in the $85,000 to $90,000 range.

May we talk?

Sincerely,

Guy M. De Marco

Guy M. DeMarco

GMD/tad

Enclosure

JACQUELINE E. TOYZER
412 Grammercy Drive
Kansas City, MO 64112

February 12, 1998

Mr. Nolan P. Kingcade
President
Delcrest Corporation
1050 Bethlehem Pike
Rochester, NY 14692

Dear Mr. Kingcade:

I am seeking an employment opportunity in an executive level sales, marketing or general management position that capitalizes on my capital goods and/or environmental background.

With over twenty years in industrial sales and marketing with Kenmore Electronics, refined with two corporate turnarounds and several start-up company assignments, I have been assisting high tech growth firms and troubled companies in realizing their profit potential.

My consulting practice has exposed me to the environmental services sector and given me the opportunity to start-up a hospital waste disposal business and underground storage tank and ground water remediation business. I have also assisted a petroleum distributor and contractor with an aggressive growth program and a reorganized major U.S. welding equipment manufacturer with a successful acquisition/merger.

While most of my successes have been in the marketing arena, I would welcome an opportunity in a division general management position that would capitalize on both my entrepreneurial and marketing strengths.

I will relocate with assistance, prefer the Northeast, and will leave compensation open to negotiation.

Sincerely,

Jacqueline E. Toyzer

Jacqueline E. Toyzer

JET/hma

Enclosure

BRENT C. THURMAN
314 Centennial Drive
Smithfield, VA 23430
(804) 357-6081

May 14, 1999

Mr. Cyrus V. Moser
President
The Haagen-Dazs Company
Glenpoint Center East
Teaneck, NJ 07666

Dear Mr. Moser:

If you are seeking a top-flight Chief Financial Officer, perhaps I may fit the bill.

In February of 1993, just after the market crash, I was successful in securing an investment grade rating on a $160 million debt for SnackWell Foods, the first time in the company's history - this was accomplished without the Canadian parent's credit support. In 1995, I successfully refinanced $110 million of acquisition debt for a U.S. subsidiary of Hostess Foods. It allowed them to sell the company for a premium.

During my tenure as senior or chief financial officer with past employers, I have developed several new credit facilities through both private and public sources. In some cases, these have been quite unique. For instance, the first insured, unleveraged multi-property real estate investment deal for the food franchising industry was masterminded by me. This business has grown to over $3.6 billion of assets now under management. I have employed captive lending facilities to improve investor returns as well as tax advantaged concepts like money market preferred stock. Of course, more traditional means like commercial paper and direct bank borrowing have been sourced as well.

I have one of those interesting business backgrounds with successful experience in manufacturing, distribution, financial services and retail. For nineteen years, cash flow improvement, whether through financing, cost containment/reduction, or revenue enhancement, has been a consistent result of my efforts in all of my business endeavors.

I have decided to seek a better opportunity. Although I am far more interested in an intriguing challenge and a good company then merely making money, you should know that in recent years my total compensation has been in the $140,000 to $160,000 range.

Should you be seeking a senior financial officer with my credentials, Mr. Moser, I would very much appreciate the chance to meet with you. Thank you for your consideration.

Sincerely,

Brent C. Thurman

Brent C. Thurman

BCT/gl

Enclosure

KATHLEEN B. SCHEIGH

1018 Fairview Knoll
Brook Park, OH 44142

Home: (316) 229-8044
Office: (316) 984-0720

July 17, 1998

Mr. Charles D. Pemberton
Director of Procurement
Allstar Plastics, Inc.
3041 Skyway Circle
Irving, TX 7538

Dear Mr. Pemberton:

I have six years of increasing responsibility as a Purchasing professional, including two years as a manager reporting to the Division Manager of Sebastian Company's hair-care products business. A sampling of some of my key accomplishments includes:

- Saved $800,000 in raw materials costs in ten months for an established
  brand through supplier contract re-negotiations

- Consolidated purchasing for polywrap and negotiated national contract
  producing over $1.2 million annual savings

- Installed JIT computer system cutting spare parts inventory requirements
  and saving $1/2 million annually in inventory investment

- Initiated changes in folding carton specification that increased
  packaging functionality and cut vital supplies inventory investment
  by $220,000 annually.

The enclosed resume will provide you with further particulars on contributions that I have made to my employer. Perhaps Foster General Corporation may wish to capitalize on my creativity and energy as well. If so, I can be reached at either my office or home telephone numbers listed above.

I hope that we will have the opportunity to discuss my qualifications further during a personal meeting. Thank you for your consideration.

Very truly yours,

Kathleen B. Scheigh

Kathleen B. Scheigh

KBS/daz

Enclosure

J. ROBERT SWEENEY
810 Farnam Street
Greenville, SC 29602

September 15, 1998

Mr. Christopher B. Reese
Director of Employment
Mosinee Paper Company
11830 Westline Industrial Park
Mosinee, W I54455-9099

Dear Mr. Reese:

I have been employed with Bowater Paper & Pulp Group for the last three years, and have decided to make a change. I am originally from the Milwaukee area, and would like the opportunity to return to Wisconsin.

I noted that Mosinee Paper was undergoing considerable expansion, with plans to add three plants and a research center over the next three years. This suggests that you will be needing to recruit the technical and operations personnel to staff this major expansion. Perhaps I can be of help.

I hold a B.A. degree in Business from Western Michigan University and have three years of experience as Technical Employment Manager with Bowater Paper & Pulp. As such, I have responsibility for all technical and operations staffing for the company, including the Technology Center and six manufacturing plants. During the last two years alone, I have recruited and successfully filled 150 technical and/or operations professional and managerial positions.

Some key accomplishments include:

- Staffed over 200 professional and managerial positions in three years

- Reduced employee turnover by 30% through implementation of improved interviewing and selection techniques

- Reduced interview-to-hire ratio by 28%, saving over $50,000 per year in candidate travel expenses

- Reduced recruiting time by 50% through implementation of creative recruiting strategies

If you will be needing an experienced employment professional who has first-hand knowledge of technical and operations recruiting in the paper industry, you may want to give me a call. I am sure that I can provide the kind of recruiting support that will be required by Mosinee Paper to successfully meet its staffing requirements and achieve its expansion objectives.

Thank you for your consideration.

Sincerely,

J. Robert Sweeney

J. Robert Sweeney

Enclosure

BETH A. FERGUESON

622 Appleford Lane
Scranton, PA 17652

Office: (717) 576-3116
Home: (717) 944-4081

February 16, 1998

Mr. Leonard S. Weinstein
Vice President Marketing
Tri-State Property Development
One Liberty Place, 36th Floor
New York, NY 10221

Dear Mr. Weinstein:

I am seeking a challenging real estate business development sales and marketing position with an organization who can effectively use my knowledge and skills. My professional business career exhibits a record of strong achievement and significant contributions. The enclosed resume details my experience and accomplishments.

During my four years of highly successful business development and sales & marketing experience, I have been recognized for my creative spirit and ability to identify and implement profitable projects. The following highlights some of my career achievements:

- Arranged financing for acquisition and development costs and prepared all
  necessary pro forma and cash flow analysis for a $6 million commercial
  development project

- Implemented successful sales and marketing plan to establish a strong presence
  for a Central Pennsylvania office of a Philadelphia-based development company

- Sold over $22 million in aggregate real estate leaseholds (56) during first 24
  months (over 5 million square feet of commercial/industrial real estate)

- Obtained all necessary approvals for a 300 unit residential subdivision

If my qualifications are of interest to you, I would welcome the chance to meet with you personally and further explore career opportunities at Tri-State Property Development. Thank you for considering my qualifications.

Sincerely,

Beth A. Fergueson

Beth A. Fergueson

Enclosure

KEITH R. COLLINS, Ph.D.

670 Union Street
Monroe, GA 30655

February 14, 1999

Dr. Alfred J. Lloyd
Director Research & Development
Armor-All Products Corporation
Six Westside Avenue
Upland, IN 46989

Dear Dr. Lloyd:

I am seeking a challenging position in chemistry in the paints and coatings, chemical, petroleum, or rubber industry. My interests, education and experience qualify me particularly in the areas of product development, quality control, chemical safety and handling of hazardous substances.

My innovative and successful career has centered around formulation, characterization, and physical testing of polymer coatings, elastomers and fibers. My knowledge of many laboratory instruments, experience in customer service, public speaking, and technical presentations should prove valuable assets.

After you have reviewed my resume, I would appreciate the opportunity to discuss my credentials and how I might contribute to Armor-All Products and its technical objectives.

Thank you.

Sincerely,

Keith R Collins

Keith R. Collins

KRC/dan

Enclosure

NORMAN A. CARTWRIGHT

176 Breezewood Estates, Sacramento, CA 95814

April 28, 1998

Mr. Wayne A. Higgins
Director of Marketing
Precision Instruments, Inc.
1920 Fifth Street
Davis, CA 95616

Dear Mr. Higgins:

Your review of my enclosed resume will be appreciated.

Briefly, I am a senior sales representative with broad program management experience and a technical background in process control and measurement as applied to production, transmission, and distribution of electricity and various industrial processes.

Should you have a suitable requirement that is appropriate to my experience, please contact me by phone at (916) 442-1733. I would be pleased to meet with you at your convenience.

Very truly yours,

Norman A. Cartwright

Enclosure

ANGELO S. MARUCCI
212 Piccolo Street
Petersburg, VA 23219
(804) 487-9167

April 23, 1998

Mr. William J. Cumberland
Regional Sales Manager
Font Master Software Inc.
2000 South Central Boulevard
Virginia Beach, VA 23454

Dear Mr. Cumberland:

As the Regional Sales Manager for one of America's premiere software companies, I am sure you are always on the lookout for outstanding sales talent. Should you, or one of the other Font Master sales regions, currently be in the market for a proven sales leader with an excellent record of achievement, you may want to give me a call.

My qualifications include a B.A. in Marketing from Ohio State and four years in technical sales with Compu-Data Corporation in the East Coast region. Some highlights of my career include:

> Doubled territory sales volume in four years time ($2 to $4 million).

> Increased new accounts from 350 to over 700.

> Won annual regional sales contest two years in a row

My full resume is enclosed for your reference.

I feel that career growth opportunities at Compu-Data are somewhat limited, and I have made a decision to seek a sales position with a more progressive company offering greater opportunity for upward mobility. Compensation requirements are in the $55,000 to $60,000 range plus company automobile.

If you feel my credentials are of interest, I would welcome a call and the opportunity to interview with your firm. I can normally be reached at my home after 7:00 p.m.

Thank you for your consideration.

Sincerely,

Angelo S Marucci

Angelo S. Marucci

Encl.

MARTHA D. ADAMSON
576 Glenside Avenue
Des Moines, IA 50313
(515) 262-3406

July 29, 1997

Mr. Noel G. Franks
Director of Manufacturing
Scientific Glass Products, Inc.
Beeker Street
Windom, MN 56101

Dear Mr. Franks:

I am interested in exploring career opportunities in operations management with Scientific Glass Products, and have therefore enclosed my resume for your reference. Should you be in the market for a young, results-oriented manufacturing manager for one of your plants, I would encourage you to consider my credentials.

A 1992 graduate of Iowa State University with a B.S. degree in Industrial Engineering, I have just over five years manufacturing experience in the glass industry with Wheaton Glass. During this time, I advanced from Shift Supervisor - Furnace Operations to Operations Manager of a 400 employee pharmaceutical glass manufacturing operation.

Some of my major contributions include:

- Successful installation and start-up of a $25 million glass manufacturing line (on time & under budget)

- Automated packaging department resulting in 30% reduction in labor costs ($4 million annual savings)

- Redesigned work assignments for finishing department and initiated skills training, resulting in 20% increase in department productivity

My strong contributions in manufacturing, coupled with solid knowledge of glass manufacturing operations, should make me an attractive candidate for an operations management assignment with your company. Should you agree, I would welcome the opportunity to meet with you and further explore this possibility.

Thank you for considering my qualifications, and I look forward to hearing from you.

Sincerely,

Martha D. Adamson

Martha D. Adamson

Enclosure

ARTHUR D. BOWES

240 Mockingbird Lane, Cass City, MI 48726

February 26, 1997

Mr. Lawrence S. Solomon
Director of Logistics
Vulcan Oil Corporation
1818 Metroplex Drive
Dallas, TX 75265-5907

Dear Mr. Solomon:

As Director of Logistics for a major oil company, I'm sure you are keenly aware of the financial contributions that a skilled Distribution Manager can make to the corporate bottom line. It is for this reason you may wish to pay particular attention to my employment qualifications as highlighted on the enclosed resume.

My credentials include a B.A. degree in Business Administration from the University of Michigan and over 15 years experience in distribution and distribution management in the chemical process and petrochemical industry. I am currently Distribution Manager for the Lubes Division of Pennzoil Corporation.

Selected accomplishments include:

- Implemented regional warehousing concept, consolidating 12 warehouses into five regional centers ($8 million annual savings).

- Automated three regional warehouses allowing for unitized handling of finished product and reducing product damage by 60% (annual savings of $2 million)

- Negotiated national truck fleet maintenance contract, reducing maintenance costs by 20% ($1.8 million annual savings).

I am seeking a senior position in distribution management at either the corporate or division level. Compensation requirements are in the $75,000 to $85,000 range.

Should you have an appropriate management opening, I would welcome the opportunity to meet with you personally to explore the contributions that I could make to your distribution operations.

Thank you for your review of my qualifications, and I look forward to your reply.

Sincerely,

Arthur D. Bowes

Arthur D. Bowes

Enclosure

MONICA C. HEINTZ

901 St. John's Drive
Hampton, NH 03842

Home: (603) 334-6521
Office: (603) 929-4700

August 26, 1998

Mr. Kenneth J. Schroeder
Director of Engineering
Groundwater Technologies
405 Frontier Plaza
Danbury, CT 06833

Dear Mr. Schroeder:

Preliminary research of your company indicates that your firm is engaged in handling large-scale engineering and start-up projects in the waste treatment field. In particular, I am quite interested in the work that you are doing in the area of site remediation. This is a field in which I have some strong expertise.

As the enclosed resume will demonstrate, I am a degreed engineer with some ten years' experience in project engineering management of large-scale site remediation projects. During the last four years, in fact, I have been Site Remediation Engineering Manager for the Roy F. Weston Company, and have directed some of Weston's largest projects for the Environmental Protection Agency.

I am thoroughly versed in all aspects of site remediation including both site evaluation and analysis as well as on-site management of the remediation process itself. I am also familiar with a wide range of remediation technologies including low- and high-temperature thermal treatment systems.

In addition to my project management expertise, I am considered a key resource to the marketing group in the sale of Weston engineering and consulting services in the site remediation area. I have played a key role in helping to land over $85 million in site remediation engineering projects in the last two years alone.

If you are in the market for a strong engineering manager to direct and grow your site remediation business, perhaps you might want to give me a call. I have the technical, marketing and managerial expertise necessary to profitably lead a major expansion of this segment of your business, and place you in a highly competitive position in this dynamic, fast-growing market.

Thank you for your consideration, and I look forward to hearing from you shortly.

Sincerely

Monica C. Heintz

Enclosure

330 Palamino Drive
Louisville, KY 40218

March 16, 1997

Ms. Sharon A. McBryde
Creative Director
VIP Advertising
1650 Pacific Highway
Carmel, CA 90393

Dear Ms. McBryde:

Creativity is the lifeblood of the advertising profession and the core value that separates the elite agency from the mundane and boring. My clients have been anything but bored, and their advertising-driven sales revenue increases have generated more than a mild interest in what I have to offer.

Unfortunately, although my current employer enjoys a healthy cash flow generated by my creative contributions to the firm, the agency is a small family-owned operation and there appears to be little opportunity for career growth beyond my current position. This has forced me to consider other employment alternatives.

Please accept my resume in application for a management position on your creative department's staff. I am seeking the opportunity to manage a small group in the development of creative ideas for T.V. commercials and national print media advertising campaigns. Compensation requirements are in the $90,000 range.

My portfolio is replete with award-winning, sales-getting advertising campaigns for such major companies as Westinghouse, Procter & Gamble, Campbell Soup, Johnson & Johnson, and others. Through the use of my creative talents, my employer has both landed and expanded business with these key firms, with sales revenues of these firms now valued at approximately $150 million annually.

Perhaps we should meet to explore how I might put my creative energies to work for your agency. Should you agree, please contact me at my home number during week nights after 8:00 p.m.

Thank you for your consideration.

Very truly yours,

Regina D. Lennox

Regina D. Lennox

Enclosure

Elizabeth A. Larkin

741 Rambling Way   Res: (602) 484-0332
Phoenix, AZ 85023   Bus: (602) 693-0800

July 12, 1999

Mr. Warren S. Dithers
Director of Procurement
Coordinated Apparel, Inc.
5760 West 96th Street
Los Angeles, CA 90040

Dear Mr. Dithers:

Enclosed please find my resume as application for the position of Senior Buyer with your firm. Review of my credentials will quickly confirm that I am a skilled and hard-working procurement professional with a propensity for continuous improvement and a real knack for returning profit to the bottom line.

Some of my noteworthy contributions include:

- Consolidated corporate-wide purchases of key chemicals resulting in volume discount and $5 million annual savings.

- Initiated blanket order system with five-hour guaranteed delivery of key packaging materials, reducing raw material inventory by 74% and resulting in $1.6 million annual savings.

- Secured 10% price reduction in purchase of all rayon fiber from major supplier (annual savings of $1.1 million).

I feel confident that I can bring similar cost savings to Coordinated Apparel as well.

My qualifications include a B.S. degree in Chemistry from the University of Southern California and six years of highly successful raw materials and packaging procurement for a well-known manufacturer of nonwoven fabrics. I have been continuously recognized by my employer for outstanding performance and can furnish excellent references upon request.

Should you have a need for a strong procurement professional, I hope that you would give me a call. Thank you for considering my credentials, and I look forward to your reply.

Sincerely,

Elizabeth A. Larkin

Elizabeth A. Larkin

Enclosure

PAUL C. GIFFORD

909 Allendale Avenue
Springford, Pennsylvania 19803
(215) 655-9153

September 23, 1998

Mr. Stanley D. Humphries
Manager of MIS
Hercules, Inc.
Market Street Towers, East
Philadelphia, PA 19102

Dear Mr. Humphries:

I heard some rumors through some of my industry contacts that Hercules is considering installation of a computerized MRP system throughout its Specialty Products Division. If you're looking for a project leader or senior systems analyst for this project, I would be an ideal candidate.

My credentials include a B.S. in Computer Science from Drexel University and over 10 years of experience as a systems analyst with Titan Chemical Company in Cherry Hill. Titan, as you may be aware, is a $560 million manufacturer of specialty chemicals sold to the agricultural chemicals industry. Currently, I hold the position of Senior Systems Analyst.

Of particular interest should be the fact that I have spent the last two years as the lead systems analyst in the installation and successful start-up of a computerized MRP system at Titan. This project was highly successful, and was completed ahead of time and on budget.

The Vice President of Manufacturing has stated that this was the most successful system installation that he has ever witnessed at Titan. The start-up was practically flawless, and the transition from manual system to computer was accomplished without missing a beat. The success of this project resulted in my receipt of a $5,000 special bonus in recognition of my contribution as the lead systems analyst.

I am enclosing a copy of my resume so that you might become familiar with the specifics of my qualifications and experience.

Should you have an interest in pursuing my candidacy, I would be pleased to hear from you. I can be reached at my home most evenings between the hours of 7:30 and 10:00 p.m.

Thank you for your consideration.

Sincerely,

Paul C. Gifford

Paul C. Gifford

Enclosure

3

Letters to Search Firms

Search firms and employment agencies are statistically known to be important sources for use in a job search. Surveys show that these firms account for 10 to 15 percent of all professional and managerial jobs found by job seekers. These studies also demonstrate that such organizations are the second most productive source; only networking (personal contact) is more successful. These facts should be remembered when you design your job-hunting campaign.

In planning your job search, target search firms and/or employment agencies as key sources of job leads. Since most of these firms will not accept unsolicited telephone calls from job seekers, it is impractical to think of maximizing the use of this important job source by calling or by walking in the door unexpectedly. This leaves only one practical means for accessing these firms—use of a direct-mail campaign.

Our firm, Brandywine Consulting Group, has experimented with direct mail to search firms and employment agencies as a job search method. To date, results have shown that 3 to 5 percent of the targeted firms will respond with an interest in the candidate. These statistics seem to hold true for professional through upper-middle-management positions. There is, however, a significant drop-off in response rate for person in senior executive positions (those at the top 5 percent of executive earnings levels).

If you are at the professional through upper-middle-management level, it is probably well worth your while to use a mass-mail approach in contacting these firms. In fact, even senior-level executives will want to use this technique. However, senior-level executives should not have unrealistic expectations concerning the number of positive responses they will receive. Mailing to 500 or 600 search firms/employment agencies should yield 15 to 30 favorable responses. In other words, 15 to 30 of the firms targeted through the mailing are likely to call to discuss a particular employment opening with one of their client companies.

In one recent Brandywine Consulting Group mailing to some 800 companies, for example, the candidate for whom we made the mailing received approximately 24 such calls. These calls resulted in 7 or 8 interviews and 3 job offers, one of which the candidate accepted. All of this activity occurred within 37 work days from initiation of this individual's job-hunting campaign.

This example demonstrates that the direct-mail campaign, aimed at search firms and employment agencies, can prove to be a very powerful job-search technique. A good broadcast cover letter can help facilitate the effectiveness of this job-hunting method.

PURPOSE OF COVER LETTER

The type of broadcast cover letter employed in a mass mailing to search firms is somewhat different from that used in a similar mailing to employers. The difference has to do with the roles of these two organizations.

The motivation of employers is to find uniquely qualified individuals who can "add value" to their organizations. As a result, it is believed that employers will read the cover letter more thoroughly than the search firm or employment agency. Employers will generally look more broadly at the candidate's overall qualifications.

By contrast, the search firm or employment agency's role is to match the candidate's qualifications with the specifics of the employer's requirements. Rather than looking at the candidate's broader credentials in a cover letter, it is believed that most third parties frequently skip the cover letter and go right to the resume to facilitate this qualifications comparison.

Additionally, search firms and employment agencies have come to realize that cover letters and resumes are frequently redundant. Why waste time reading the cover letter before establishing that an appropriate match exists through comparison of the candidate's resume and the client's candidate specification? This is not to say that these firms won't read the cover letter at all. Most, in fact, do—but only after determining that there is an appropriate fit with their client's needs.

Search firms and employment agencies view the cover letter principally as a "letter of transmittal." They consider its primary purpose to be a vehicle for transmitting the candidate's resume, as opposed to a document that adds any real value to the selection/comparison process. Thus, there is much less likelihood that the candidate can effectively use the cover letter to sell the search firm or agency or his or her value. The cover letter, when sent directly to employers, is believed to be better received, thereby increasing the probability that the candidate will be offered an interview based on key factors contained in the cover letter.

KEY LETTER ELEMENTS

Because the purpose of cover letters sent to search firms and employment agencies is principally that of "resume transmittal," these letters tend to be relatively brief compared to the broadcast letters sent directly to employers. The principal difference between the two is that the search firm/employment agency letter places less emphasis on selling specific value and more emphasis on providing a general, overall summary of qualifications.

The following are key elements normally found in the search firm/employment agency broadcast cover letter:

1. First paragraph contains:
   a. Statement of job search objective (position sought);
   b. Request to be considered for firm's current and future job search assignments.
2. Second paragraph contains an overall "qualifications summary" including:
   a. Educational credentials;
   b. Relevant work experience.
3. Third paragraph contains a "statement of appreciation" for the firm's review and consideration of the applicant's qualifications.

In addition to the above "standard" paragraphs, authors of these types of cover letters may choose to include one or more of the following paragraphs:

1. Explanation of reason for making career change.
2. A "selling" or "value-adding" paragraph citing key accomplishments relevant to job search objective.
3. Statement specifying compensation requirements.
4. Statement specifying geographical preferences or restrictions.
5. Statement providing contact instructions.

The balance of this chapter provides a wide selection of well-written search firm cover letters that should facilitate your design of an effective letter for use in your job-hunting campaign.

GREGORY A. NORTON

7 Michigan Avenue, Dundee, Illinois 60118

June 18, 1998

Mr. Peter J. Gavin
The Northland Agency
5667 Fritztown Road
Minneapolis, MN 55426

Dear Mr. Gavin:

I understand from some of my associates that your agency specializes in placing technical personnel in the electronics field. Perhaps you are currently working on an assignment for one of your clients which might align well with my qualifications and requirements.

I am seeking a position as a Programmer Analyst providing technical programming support to Development Engineers in the development of state-of-the-art communications controllers or related technology. Key qualifications include:

- M.S. degree in Computer Science

- Three years technical programming support experience in an R&D electronics environment

- In-depth knowledge of the SNA/ACP/NCP functions of a communications controller in a PEP environment

- Proficiency in SNA/ACP/NCP internals

- Proficiency with SDLC, various trace facilities, ALC and TSO/WYLBUR/SPF

- Expert in use of data analyzer equipment

My current compensation is $58,000 and I have no geographical restrictions.

Should you be aware of a suitable opportunity, I would appreciate hearing from you. Thank you for your consideration.

Sincerely,

Gregory A. Norton

Gregory A. Norton

Enclosure

WILLIAM A. BARLOW
1622 Poinsettia Street
Richmond, VA 29202-1752

March 30, 1998

Mr. Ronald L. Wise
Management Recruiters, Inc.
30 Woodstock Street
Roswell, GA 30075

Dear Mr. Wise:

Could one of your client companies use an ambitious, young accounting professional with an excellent record of growth and accomplishment as an accounting supervisor?

I am thoroughly trained and ready for my first supervisory assignment. I have a solid technical foundation in accounting fundamentals, which I gained during my last three years of employment at Precision Electronics, Inc. In addition, I have strong interpersonal, communications and leadership skills, which should serve me well in a supervisory role.

Beyond my professional experience, I hold both a B.A. and M.B.A. from Syracuse University, where I majored in accounting. As my resume will attest, I was both a scholar and a campus leader.

Although I would prefer to remain in the east, I will give serious consideration to other locations, should the opportunity be a good one.

Should you identify a suitable opportunity for me, Mr. Wise, I can be reached on a confidential basis at my office during the day or at my home during evening hours. Both phone numbers are on the enclosed resume.

Thank you.

Sincerely,

William A. Barlow

William A. Barlow

Enclosure

THOMAS C. WOOD

1808 Skyline Drive   (412) 977-8104
Pittsburgh, PA 14332   (412) 323-4076

July 22, 1999

Mr. Willard B. Travis
Travis & Co., Inc.
325 Boston Post Road
Sudbury, MA 01776

Dear Mr. Travis:

For the past several years, I have been running the Chemicals Business for
General Industries, Inc. In late 1997, that business was sold to Dow
Chemical Company. I am now in the process of a career change.

I understand that your company services the chemical industry and thought
I would forward a copy of my resume for your information and review.

If you know of any opportunities, I would appreciate being considered.
Should you require additional information or need to discuss my
qualifications in more detail, please give me a call. Thank you in advance
for your time and consideration.

Sincerely,

Thomas C Wood

Thomas C. Wood

TCW/dn

Enclosure

FAYE M. ANDERSON
133 Sheffield Avenue
Inverness, FL 32650
(814) 357-9018

October 10, 1998

Mr. George L. Resinger
Sigma Group, Inc.
600 17th Street, Ste. 1440
Brentwood, TN 37207

Dear Mr. Resinger:

I am seeking a project engineering position in the metals industry. My research indicates that your firm services clients in the metals and related industries, so I am enclosing my resume for your review and consideration.

I am an ambitious, young Senior Project Engineer with five years experience in the design, installation and start-up of aluminum manufacturing processes and equipment. I have strong engineering skills and have earned an excellent reputation for project timeliness and cost efficiency. The following are some of my key accomplishments:

- Managed mechanical design of $20 million aluminum furnace complex (completed on time and under budget).

- Redesigned refractory lining in a flash calciner process to reduce heat loss by 30% in existing units and 50% in new units. (Potential savings $4.5 million annually).

- Directed design and installation of $12 million furnace and associated material handling equipment. (Completed two months ahead of schedule and 15% under budget).

Should one of your client companies be in search of a results-oriented, highly motivated senior project engineer with my credentials, I would appreciate the opportunity to further discuss my qualifications with you.

My geographical preference is in the Southwestern United States, and my compensation requirements are in the low $70,000 range.

Thank you for your consideration, and I look forward to hearing from you.

Very truly yours,

Faye M. Anderson

Faye M. Anderson

FMA:jdg

Enclosure

DENNIS M. RUSSELL

1427 Alberta Drive
Cleveland, OH 44115

Home: (316) 898-4051
Office: (316) 477-9161

September 12, 1998

Ms. Kathleen O'Callaghan
O'Callaghan & Associates Inc.
1127 Euclid Avenue, Ste. 375
Ft. Worth, TX 76109

Dear Ms. O'Callaghan:

I am taking this opportunity to write to you regarding career opportunities that may exist within your client community.

My current position is Director of Systems Development with Computer World Stores in Cleveland, Ohio, and I was previously with the Information Services Division of Carter Hawley Hale Stores in Anaheim, California.

I have in excess of 20 years of experience in retail systems development within the MIS organizations, which includes major accomplishments in systems development, data administration, data center computer operations, information center and quality assurance departments.

Although I'm far more interested in finding a good company and an interesting opportunity, you will want to be aware that my annual compensation has been in the $125,00 to $130,000 range during the last few years.

I look forward to having the opportunity to more fully describe my qualifications, should you have a suitable assignment for which you wish to consider me. Thank you.

Sincerely,

Dennis M. Russell

Dennis M. Russell

Enclosure

FRANCIS J. MADDEN

610 Newport Drive, Hampden, Maine 04644

May 13, 1998

Mr. Robert C. Grecco
Grecco, Divine & Co., Inc.
4100 International Plaza
Tower II, Ste. 600
New York, NY 10017

Dear Mr. Grecco:

I am writing to you in hopes that you are currently providing service to client firms seeking uniquely talented claims management or operations professionals for the insurance industry. With a consistent track record of success within both the property and casualty and managed healthcare industries, I believe that I could contribute immediately to a variety of claims and operational issues.

I have enclosed my resume to provide you with the details of my background and skills. I would be most anxious to discuss my career goals with you -- even if on a purely exploratory basis.

If you have any immediate questions, do not hesitate to call. Should you have employment opportunities which you feel may be of interest to me, I would appreciate hearing from you. My home phone number is (207) 848-5693.

Thank you for your consideration, and I look forward to hearing from you.

Sincerely,

Francis J Madden

Francis J. Madden

Enclosure

KAREN E. ASHBY
21734 Ventura Blvd, Apt. 450
Woodland Hills, CA 91363
(408) 622-3489

April 14, 1998

Ms. Judith T. McCall
McCall Resources
1511 Sansome Street, 21st Floor
San Francisco, CA 94104

Dear Ms. McCall:

Enclosed please find my resume for your review and consideration against either current or future search assignments in the field of Human Resources.

I am seeking a responsible and challenging corporate or division level position as a human resource generalist. Consideration would also be given to a position in the field of Labor Relations.

My salary requirements are in the $75,000 range with flexibility dependent upon area, future opportunity and other similar factors. Although I have no absolute geographical restrictions, I do have a strong preference for the West and Southwest areas.

Thank you for your consideration, and I look forward to the prospect of discussing appropriate career opportunities with you or a member of your staff.

Sincerely,

Karen E. Ashby

Karen E. Ashby

KEA:seb

Enclosure

FREDERICK A. LIVINGSTON

2110 Alabaster Avenue
Lapeer, MI 48446

Home: (603) 227-6113
Office: (603) 762-6315

May 25, 1999

Mr. Lee Koehn
Lee Koehn Associates, Inc.
250 Route 28, Ste. 206
Bridgewater, NJ 08807

Dear Mr. Koehn:

I am seeking challenging opportunities in Operations Management at the corporate, division, or major operating level. Perhaps one of your current or future clients may be looking for a strong Operations Executive and have an interest in my qualifications.

As my resume shows, I have had excellent career progression in the field of Operations Management at both DuPont and Dow Chemical Company. Unfortunately, the division for which I have been working has been sold and my position as Director of Operations has been eliminated.

You will note from my resume that I have established an excellent track record for generating overall cost reduction and operation efficiency improvements for each of my past employers. I take particular pride in staying current with new approaches and methodologies for improving operations, and am quick to apply those that will generate solid bottom line results.

If one of your clients seeks a highly motivated Operations Executive with strong leadership skills and a demonstrated record for running efficient and profitable operations, perhaps you will think of me.

I can be reached, during the day or evening, at the numbers listed on this letterhead.

Very truly yours,

Frederick A. Livingston

Frederick A. Livingston

FAL:pl

Enclosure

ROSE MARIE DOYLE

501 Cambridge Street
Boston, MA 02141

Home: (617) 676-3150
Office: (617) 297-6363

December 3, 1997

Mr. David R. Biren
Senior Partner
The Biren Agency, Inc.
14 S. Park Street
Montclair, NJ 07042

Dear Mr. Biren:

I am a results-oriented, senior level marketing executive with over 14 years experience in all phases of marketing and sales management. Innovativeness has proven to be my greatest asset, and I am credited with substantial increases in overall sales volume for each of my past employers as a result of the fresh new market approaches and creative ideas that I have contributed to these organizations.

The following are some of my key accomplishments:

- Catapulted company to Number 1 in sales in European specialty resins market in only two years (33% increase in export sales)

- Led national roll-out of new low viscosity resin product with resultant $58 million sales in first year

- Repositioned old brand through creative advertising approach that revitalized product and resulted in 150% increase in sales volume in six months

- Replaced independent manufacturers representative network with direct sales force, reducing cost-of-sales 30% over three year period

- Directed installation of order tracking computer system that led to reduction in order delivery time of 23% in 18 months.

My enclosed resume further details my extensive experience and qualifications as a marketing executive.

Should one of your specialty chemicals clients be in the market for a top-flight marketing and sales executive as a member of their senior management team, perhaps you will give my qualifications serious consideration. My marketing knowledge, creativity and energy could prove a valuable asset in helping them to realize their full growth potential.

Thank you for your time and consideration.

Sincerely,

Rose Marie Doyle

Rose Marie Doyle

Enclosure

233 Westheimer Lane
Norwalk, CT 06854

July 5, 1997

Ms. Brenda C. Hawkins
The Hawkins Group
2340 Orrington Avenue
Portland, ME 20116

Dear Ms. Hawkins:

I am a senior human resources executive with over 15 years experience. Currently, I am Director of Corporate Staff Human Resources for Hanson Paper Company, a $5.5 billion, Fortune 200 consumer products company.

Although Hanson has generally been good to me, I have some concerns about future career progression due to a long-term strategy designed to reduce the size of the corporate staff organization. This consolidation, coupled with the relatively young age of the top human resource executives, suggests that future career progression at the senior levels will be severely limited in the short to intermediate term. I have thus opted to confidentially explore other career options outside of the company.

My qualifications include an M.B.A. from Michigan State University with an emphasis in Human Resource Management. My career progression at Hanson has included human resource management assignments at the corporate, division and manufacturing plant level. I am well schooled and heavily seasoned in a wide range of human resource functions, including: organization design, management development, employment, compensation and benefits, and labor relations.

I am seeking a senior human resources position at the vice-presidential level, with full responsibility for all human resource functions. Compensation requirements are in the six figure range, and I am open to relocation to most parts of the U.S.

Should one of your clients be in the market for a senior-level human resources executive with my credentials, I would appreciate a call. Thank you for your consideration.

Sincerely,

Vincent J. Hartman

Vincent J. Hartman

Enclosure

WALLACE D. POLK, Ph.D.

510 Monroe Street
Evanston, IL 60201
(312) 437-9736

January 13, 1997

Mr. Stephen Goldram
Stephen Goldram Search Consultants, Inc.
P. O. Box 33
Gary, IL 60013

Dear Mr. Goldram:

I am a Ph.D. organic chemist from Columbia University with 12 years of experience in R&D and R&D management, and also hold an MBA with three years experience in business development and analysis including acquisitions, foreign joint ventures and strategic planning.

My areas of technical expertise are polymer composites, adhesives, polymer chemistry in unsaturated polyester, vinyl ester, urethane and epoxy, fine organic chemicals, petrochemicals, and homogeneous and heterogeneous catalysis.

I am capable of handling a wide spectrum of business development projects ranging from new application/product development and new market development, to creating entirely new businesses, to strategic expansion via acquisition and joint venture.

I am seeking a management position in a technology-oriented polymer chemical company in business/market development or research and development, where I can fully utilize both my technical and business expertise to create new business opportunities for my employer.

I am willing to relocate, and would consider positions paying in excess of $80,000 per year.

If you are aware of a suitable employment opportunity with one of your clients, I would appreciate hearing from you. Thank you.

Yours very truly,

Wallace D. Polk

Wallace D. Polk

Enclosure

ELAINE D. HOFFMEIR

1549 Chelsea Court   Home: (614) 745-4372
Beachwood, OH 44122   Office: (614) 997-0300

April 26, 1998

Mr. John T. Erlanger
Erlanger Associates
2 Pickwick Plaza
Greenwich, CT 06830

Dear Mr. Erlanger:

Your clients may be in search of a Total Quality Manager, who has
successfully led the implementation of an SPC-based total quality effort on a
company-wide basis. I have successfully led such an effort. Enclosed is my
resume which provides specifics of my qualifications.

OBJECTIVE:	Corporate Manager - Total Quality
LOCATION:	Northeastern United States
COMPENSATION:	$70,000 to $75,000
TRAVEL:	Up to 60% Acceptable

Should you require further information, I can be reached at the phone numbers
listed above.

Thank you.

Sincerely,

Elaine D. Hoffmeir

Elaine D. Hoffmeir

Enclosure

EUGENE A. DROMESHAUSER

1014 Old Forrest Lane, Broomall, PA 19008 (610) 337-5619

April 23, 1996

Ms. Linda E. Brolin
LEB Associates, Inc.
124 N. Summit Street, Ste. 3305
Toledo, OH 43604

Dear Ms. Brolin:

Although I enjoy the challenges of my present position, I am seeking alternatives to a lengthy commute into New York City. You may have a requirement for a procurement professional with strong background in purchasing of packaging materials.

I am now Buyer - Packaging Materials for the Wharton Paper Company, a $1.6 billion manufacturer of consumer paper products and sanitary tissues. As such, I purchase over $30 million of packaging materials and vital supplies annually. This includes polywrap, folding cartons, and corrugated containers for the company's four manufacturing plants.

Enclosed is a current resume for your records. Although salary is not my first consideration, my minimum compensation requirement is $55,000.

Should my qualifications be a match for one of your needs, I would appreciate hearing from you. Thank you for your consideration.

Sincerely yours,

Eugene A. Dromeshauser

Eugene A. Dromeshauser

EAD/mmb

Enclosure

36 Winchip Road
Princeton, NJ 08979

August 12, 1998

Ms. Dana Willis
The Corporate Source Group
1 Cranberry Hill
Lexington, MA 021743

Dear Ms. Willis:

I am an accomplished sales professional with four years experience in selling complex business systems to a variety of business applications. My enclosed resume will detail the specifics of my experience and accomplishments, however, I would like to highlight the fact that I have been the Top Regional Sales Representative for the Eastern Region for the last three years running.

I am seeking a senior sales or district sales management position selling "big ticket" business systems (i.e., computers, mailing systems, microfilm systems, etc.) to governmental agencies, manufacturing and/or services businesses. I especially enjoy selling complex systems that require applications problem solving for marketing success. This is an area of particular strength for me, and one which I find very satisfying.

Briefly, my qualifications include a B.S. degree in Psychology from the University of Maryland and four years selling microfilm systems for the Berry Corporation. During this period, I have increased sales in my territory by 150% and have replaced competition at several leading accounts. Major customers include: the U.S. Department of Labor, the U.S. Department of the Navy, DuPont, IBM, General Dynamics and Black & Decker, to mention a few.

If any of your client companies are looking for an accomplished sales professional with a strong background in business equipment systems sales, I would welcome the opportunity to talk with them. Compensation requirements are in the $80,000 range, and I am open to relocation to most areas of the country.

Thank you for your review of my qualifications, and I hope to hear from you shortly.

Sincerely,

Christopher T. Beatty

Christopher T. Beatty

JEFFREY A. MORSE
3601 Algonquin Road
Birmingham, AL 48009

March 15, 1997

The Walker Group, Inc.
2600 Fernbrook Lane, Ste. 106
Minneapolis, MN 55447

Dear Sir/Madam:

This summer I will be completing my obligation as an officer in the United States Navy and will be making the transition to civilian employment. A complete resume detailing my qualifications is enclosed for your reference.

The following highlights my job search objectives:

EMPLOYMENT OBJECTIVE:	Engineering or engineering project management position
PREFERRED LOCATION:	Greater Philadelphia area (open to other geographical locations)
SALARY REQUIREMENTS:	Flexible -- $60,000 minimum
AVAILABILITY:	Late July, 1997

If you are aware of any positions with your client companies that would allow me to utilize and refine my engineering and/or engineering management skills, please call. I look forward to hearing from you.

Thank you.

Sincerely,

Jeffrey A. Morse

Jeffrey A. Morse

GEORGE G. ATKESON

719 Lighthouse Road
Hilton Head, SC 19928

Home: (913) 747-3127
Office: (913) 631-2077

June 1, 1998

Mr. H. G. Sloane
Sloane, Sloane & Smith
4405 Steubenville Pike
Pittsburgh, PA 15205

Dear Mr. Sloane:

I am writing to inquire about possible positions with any of your clients as a General Manager or Plant Manager in the chemical or related industries.

As Plant Manager for a large chemical company, I brought the operation from a $12 million loss to a $7 million profit in only seven years. I used TQM methods to achieve significant cost reductions and productivity improvements, via personnel training and development. A strong customer orientation and business team interaction created good market penetrating through an improved level of service and customer-focused product enhancements.

As the enclosed resume shows, I have over 15 years of extensive, diversified experience in the chemical industry. I would like to bring my proven track record for cost reduction and product development to an entrepreneurial, growing organization that can benefit from my knowledge and experience.

As a follow-up to this correspondence, I will plan to call you to determine what, if any, opportunities may exist with your clients. If no appropriate opportunities exist, I would welcome your ideas and counsel.

Thank you for your time, and I look forward to talking with you shortly.

Sincerely,

George G. Atkeson

George G. Atkeson

GGA:bas

REGINA D. LENNOX

519 Redwood Lane, Indianapolis, Indiana 66211   (603) 927-8147

June 20, 1998

Mr. Sean T. Leinwetter
M. Shirley & Associates, Inc.
2030 Fairburn Avenue, Ste. 100
Los Angeles, CA 90025

Dear Mr. Leinwetter:

I am a graduate of the Wharton School with an MBA in Finance and three years experience as a Financial Analyst with the Drummond Aerospace Corporation here in Indianapolis. I have decided to make a career change and am interested in finding a similar position with a company in the consumer products industry. Perhaps one of your clients may have an interest in my background.

The following have been some key accomplishments at Drummond:

- Developed manufacturing cost projections and funding requirements for a $200 million missile guidance project

- Secured funding for $500 million business expansion at highly favorable terms

- Developed computer model for projection of manufacturing costs for new electronic subassemblies

- Recipient of two government commendations for outstanding achievement in financial planning

I am young and ambitious, and will have an interest only in those companies who can demonstrate clear opportunities for rapid career advancement based upon knowledge and contribution to the business. Opportunities for advancement into management short-term will also be a factor in my decision.

I would prefer positions in the Midwest, with a particular interest in the Chicago area. I am open to other locations, however, dependent upon the specifics of the opportunity. Compensation requirements are in the $70,000 range.

I would hope to hear from you shortly, should you have an appropriate opportunity which you feel may be of interest to me. Thank you for your consideration.

Sincerely,

Regina D. Lennox

Regina D. Lennox

Enclosure

ANDREW S. RIDENOUR
40 Boulder Avenue
Charlestown, RI 02813

February 18, 1998

The Lowell Agency
12200 Park Central Drive
Suite 120
Dallas, TX 75251

Dear Sir/Madam:

I am an experienced Accounting executive seeking an opportunity for further career advancement in accounting/financial management. Some of my accomplishments are outlined in the enclosed resume.

My ability to creatively deal with rapid growth and to manage and develop people, in addition to technical qualifications, are well documented and should allow me to make a significant contribution to the right company.

I have no geographical restrictions. Salary requirements are negotiable as appropriate with the specific opportunity.

Since my current employer is unaware of my decision to seek other employment, I would appreciate your treating this inquiry with appropriate sensitivity. I can be reached discreetly at work, (217) 362-9171 or through my wife at home, (217) 848-4397.

Thank you for your consideration.

Sincerely,

Andrew S. Ridenour

Andrew S. Ridenour

ASR:jls

Enclosure

BRUCE T. HUNTER
136 Oak Knoll
Mountain Lakes, NJ 07046

July 11, 1998

Ms. Beverly Kiplinger
B. Kiplinger & Associates
1107 Kenilworth Drive, Ste. 208
Baltimore, MD 21204

Dear Ms. Kiplinger:

Enclosed please find my resume.

I possess a significant record of accomplishment in senior-level Marketing/Sales Management positions along with early exposure to Accounting and Finance. My experience has been gained in diverse situations ranging from new ventures and business development/acquisitions, to two highly successful turnarounds.

My objective is to continue progression in the Marketing/Sales Management field or to pursue an opportunity in General Management. I would appreciate being considered for any opportunity you deem appropriate.

Thank you in advance for your consideration. I look forward to speaking with you in the near future.

Sincerely,

Bruce T. Hunter

Bruce T. Hunter

BTH:cab

Enclosure

C. RICHARD WELSH
819 Devonshire Road
New Rochelle, NY 10804

July 16, 1998

Mr. Michael S. Silvon
Silvon & Associates
Executive Search Consultants
9 Wakefield Road, Ste. 200
Lake Bluff, IL 60044

Dear Mr. Silvon:

It has come to my attention that your firm specializes in executive search consulting in the field of Human Resources. Since I am a specialist seeking a senior-level position in Employment, it seems appropriate to forward my resume for your review against current search assignments.

As you can see from my resume, I hold an M.S. in Psychology from the University of Michigan and have over 14 years experience in the field of Human Resources with nearly 10 years in Employment. I am currently Director of Employment for Beecham Laboratories, a $1.5 billion manufacturer of proprietary pharmaceuticals. In this capacity, I manage a staff of five professionals and provide corporate-wide recruiting and internal staffing support to a five-plant, 22,000 employee organization.

My wife, Peggy, has just completed her Master's degree at Columbia's School of Engineering & Applied Science and has received an excellent employment offer from Ford Aerospace in Orlando. We both enjoy sailing and have always been attracted to the Florida area. This offers the perfect opportunity for us to make a move.

Please consider my credentials for any employment-related search assignments you are currently conducting for firms located in the Orlando or surrounding areas (up to 1-1/2 hours commute). Although I would prefer an assignment at the Director level, I realize that I may need to be flexible in order to realize my geographical objective. Minimum compensation requirements are in the mid $60,000 range.

Thank you for taking the time to review my credentials, and I look forward to hearing from you.

Sincerely,

C. Richard Welsh

C. Richard Welsh

Enclosure

MALLORY M. GREENE
766 West Rolling Road
State College, PA 15332

January 3, 1998

Ms. Violet Bradley
The Bradley Agency
40 Cutter Mill Road
Great Neck, NY 11021

Dear Ms. Bradley:

I will be receiving an MBA in Finance from the Smeal School of Business in June of this year, and am seeking a position as a Financial Analyst with a high-technology manufacturing or research company in Florida or one of the Southern Coastal States. My husband, Warren, and I are avid sailors and our objective is to be near a large body of water.

Besides graduating with honors in Finance, highlights of my qualifications include two years of employment as a Contract Cost Accountant with Belvar Electronics, Inc. and two summers of employment in the Corporate Finance Department of General Electric's Aerospace Division in Valley Forge, PA. While at GE, I handled financial projections for several classified electronics projects.

Compensation requirements are in the high $60,000 range. Should you be aware of a suitable opportunity with one of your clients, I would appreciate hearing from you.

Thank you for your consideration.

Very truly yours,

Mallory M. Greene

Mallory M. Greene

Enclosure

AGNES M. RUFENACH

310 Normandy Road   Home: (610) 739-7052
Bryn Mawr, PA 19110   Office: (610) 471-2412

May 16, 1996

Mr. Richard J. Morgan
Morgan Samuels Co., Inc.
6 Bemiston Avenue, Ste. 1212
St. Louis, MO 63105

Dear Mr. Morgan:

I am an experienced Architectural Engineer with over ten years experience in architectural design of commercial high-rise structures. Most recently, I was the Lead Engineer in the design of Liberty Place, the 62-story commercial high-rise building that now dominates the Philadelphia skyline and has won numerous national design awards.

Other major projects with which I have played a key design role include the Baltimore Aquarium, Skyline Towers (a 32 story office building in Baltimore), and Surrey Place West (a 22-story office complex in Washington, D.C.). In my 10-1/2 years in the Architectural Design field, I have won over 20 national and local awards for design excellence.

Unfortunately, Philmore Associates, Inc., the major development firm with which I have been associated since the beginning of my career, has just filed for Chapter Eleven bankruptcy and a massive reorganization of the company is now underway. It seems appropriate at this time for me to think about moving on with my career.

I am seeking a senior engineering or management position with a major developer or architectural engineering firm specializing in the design and/or construction of commercial high-rise structures. Compensation requirements are in the six figure range, and I would prefer an equity position in the firm, if available.

Relocation is no obstacle. I am quite willing to go where the opportunity is, however, I do have a preference for the Northeast. Overseas assignments will also be considered.

Should one of your clients have an appropriate position which you feel may be of interest to me, I would appreciate a call. Thank you for your consideration.

Sincerely,

Agnes M. Rufenach

Agnes M. Rufenach

Enclosure

1926 Peele Street
Sacramento, CA 94903

April 15, 1998

Mr. Paul C. Ryan
Ryan & Associates
One Northgate Drive, 2nd Floor
San Francisco, CA 94111

Dear Mr. Ryan:

I was informed by a colleague that your firm has some specialization in the placement of Materials and Logistics professionals. I am thus enclosing my resume for your consideration in light of assignments you may be working on that require someone with my credentials.

As my resume shows, I have a B.S. in Business Administration from Lafayette College and three years experience in Procurement with Sanford Pharmaceuticals here in Sacramento. Some of my key accomplishments while at Sanford are as follows:

- Saved $1.3 million through negotiation of two year contract on knock-down cartons at a price 20% below past pricing level

- Used computer analysis to adjust order cycle on polywrap, reducing inventory by 36% ($3/4 million savings annually)

- Selected, modified and installed raw material forecasting computer system allowing greater control and efficiency in accurately forecasting and planning raw materials and supplies inventory requirements

Sanford Pharmaceuticals, as you may be aware, has recently been acquired by Fenwick Corporation, a London-based pharmaceutical giant. Fenwick has announced plans to cut back on the management staff at Sanford. This does not appear to bode well for immediate career growth. Since I am early in my career and career growth is important to me, I have elected to seek opportunities elsewhere.

Should one of your clients be looking for a young ambitious Procurement professional who has a strong work ethic and a demonstrated drive for bringing continuous improvement to business systems and processes, I hope that you will contact me.

Thank you for reviewing my credentials, and I hope to hear from you in the near future.

Sincerely,

John R. Hall

John R. Hall

Enclosure

RICHARD E. INGRAM
870 Hunt Club Lane
Danville, PA 15791

March 25, 1997

The Johnson Group, Inc.
1 World Trade Center, Ste. 2020
New York, NY 10048-0202

Dear Sir/Madam:

I am an honors engineering student at Bucknell University and will be graduating with a B.S. in Mechanical Engineering in May of this year.

I am in search of an entry-level position as a Project Engineer in the central engineering department of a manufacturing company. I would enjoy being involved with the engineering, installation and start-up of manufacturing equipment as well as general plant facilities engineering work.

Besides my academic achievement, I have been active in athletics and have been a member of the Varsity Crew Team for the last three years. I have a balanced perspective and maintain involvement in a wide range of diverse activities.

Last summer I was an Engineering Intern with The Clorox Company, where I worked in their central engineering department as a Design Engineer in support of plant capital projects. Although I enjoyed working at Clorox, unfortunately there is a hiring freeze that will not allow the opportunity for employment at this time.

Should one of your client companies have room in their organization for a bright, eager, young Project Engineer, I would appreciate a call. Thank you for your time and consideration.

Sincerely,

Richard E. Ingram

Richard E. Ingram

Enclosure

EDWARD L. MASSIE
1633 Gypsy Lane
Germantown, PA 19444

September 16, 1999

Ms. Constance A. Springer
Catalyx Group, Inc.
Civic Opera Building
20 N. Wacker Drive, Ste. 3119
Chicago, IL 60606-3101

Dear Ms. Springer:

My company has recently been sold, and the new owners have chosen to manage the business themselves. I am therefore looking for a new opportunity in a senior operating role such as President & C.E.O., C.O.O., or Vice President and General Manager.

While I would prefer to remain in the medical/surgical products or consumer health and beauty aids industries, where I have been particularly successful, I would also be interested in pursuing other areas with a company interested in my experience and abilities. Additionally, I would be open to new start-up business opportunities offering a "sweat equity" position as a General Manager.

If you currently have a search assignment that fits these requirements, and you feel my background is appropriate, I would be pleased to hear from you.

My compensation requirements are in the low six figure range, and I am open to relocation for a suitable opportunity.

Thank you for your consideration.

Sincerely,

Edward L. Massie

Edward L. Massie

ELM/tad

Enclosure

EILEEN B. LANG
801 Forsyth Boulevard
Clayton, MO 63105

August 21, 1999

Mr. Anthony J. Myers
Carlyle Associates
33 Main Street
Stamford, CT 06901

Dear Mr. Myers:

Atlas Paper Company has recently announced a 25% cutback in its Technology Department. Unfortunately, as one of the least senior employees, I will be affected.

I hold a B.S. degree in Electrical Engineering from the University of Missouri and have two years experience as a Development Engineer with the Control System Development Group at Atlas. In this capacity, I work with the Process Development Group in the first-time application of computer control systems to novel, state-of-the-art papermaking and converting processes. Following are some of my accomplishments:

- Engineered entire process control system for prototype nonwoven materials manufacturing process

- Assisted Central Engineering with the first line scale-up of new diaper converting process, with responsibility for leading scale-up of distributed control systems

- Engineered motor control system for new pilot scale paper machine

I have a strong background in the design, engineering, installation and start-up of a wide range of instrumentation and control systems. I have the ability to apply this knowledge to both pilot and full-scale manufacturing equipment. I am equally at home with both chemical and mechanical process applications.

My resume is enclosed for your review. I am seeking a Control Systems Engineering position in either a plant manufacturing or research laboratory setting and would welcome the opportunity to talk with any of your client companies for whom my background and interests are an appropriate fit. Compensation requirements are in the $55,000 to $60,000 range, and I am open to opportunities with any of your clients located in the midwest.

Thank you for your consideration and I hope to hear from you in the near future.

Sincerely,

Eileen B. Lang

Eileen B. Lang

EBL:cbs

Enclosure

JOSEPH E. CLANCY

576 West Cyprus Street, Tampa, FL 33607

April 19, 1998

Ms. Judith Blumenthal
Blumenthal Partners
393 Main Street
Raleigh, NC 27615

Dear Ms. Blumenthal:

Enclosed please find my resume, which details a short but highly successful career in sales and marketing.

Currently, I am a Sales Representative in eastern Pennsylvania for Clarion Metals, a $100 million manufacturer of metal fasteners sold to the hardware trade in the Northeastern U.S.

During my first two years selling for Clarion, I have more than doubled the sales volume for my territory, going from an annual volume of $10 million to over $22 million. The company is obviously very pleased with my performance!

Unfortunately, Clarion is a family-owned company and long-range development opportunities appear rather limited. As I look at the senior-level positions within the company (Director level and above), it has become painfully obvious that being a member of the Clarion family is an absolute prerequisite. It is clear, therefore, that I must move on with my career.

Please review the enclosed resume against your current search assignments for sales and marketing personnel. I have an excellent track record and will be a strong producer for any of your clients who can use my background and experience.

Compensation requirements are in the $50,000 range, and I am receptive to relocation in the Southeastern U.S. Thank you for your consideration.

Sincerely,

Joseph E. Clancy

Joseph E. Clancy

JEC/lm

Enclosure

DONALD L. LINDERMAN
404 Plymouth Circle
Dayton, OH 45409

March 29, 1994

Mr. Roger S. Elliott
The Elliott Company
434 Greentree Center
Atlanta, GA 30328

Dear Mr. Elliott:

With today's economic environment and continued pressure on debt, cash flow, and profitability, companies need people who can make a difference.

I can help. My credentials are strong in Finance, Treasury, and Business Development/Planning. My track record demonstrates exceptional financial, business and leadership skills. For example:

*   After being asked to corral a renegade marketing group, I added numerous controls and won the confidence of marketing by being a business partner. The results -- increases of over 25% in sales and 50% in profits. Today, we are taking ownership of additional product lines with a target of $290 million.

*   After the merger, I was asked to redesign the cash management network and U.S. order review process. The results -- $37 million annual savings, tighter controls, and greater customer satisfaction.

*   Worked closely with investment bankers to develop innovative financing and investment programs. The results -- savings of $1.3 million per year.

Now I seek a new, more challenging career option. I can produce similar results elsewhere, perhaps for one of your valued clients.

If I am a fit for one of your current search assignments, I welcome the opportunity to meet with you. Thank you for your consideration.

Sincerely,

Donald L Linderman

Donald L. Linderman

Enclosure

GLORIA D. WYATT

541 Cumberland Avenue, Houston, TX 77042

October 15, 1999

Mr. Thomas MacCarthy
Empire Executive Search
1147 Lancaster Avenue
Berwyn, PA 19312

Dear Mr. MacCarthy:

Enclosed is my updated resume which outlines my 15+ years experience in MIS.

The focus of my career has been on the development, implementation and integration of management information systems in four major industries: Health Care, Government, Retail and Manufacturing.

I can provide numerous references from both my current employer, as well as current and past clients, regarding my achievements and contributions.

Please contact me at my office (703) 644-3039 or home (703) 557-7049 with any questions you may have concerning my qualifications.

Thank you for your consideration, and I look forward to hearing from you regarding appropriate opportunities that may exist with your clients.

Sincerely,

Gloria D. Wyatt

Gloria D. Wyatt

Enclosure

FLORENCE G. STEVENS

101 Bayhill Drive   Home: (904) 928-1736
Jacksonville, FL 32202   Office: (904) 279-3000

May 12, 1998

Mr. James A. Hayden
Hayden Group, Inc.
10 High Street
Boston, MA 02110

Dear Mr. Hayden:

During the past eight years I have played a major role in revitalizing the chemicals and specialties businesses of the Worthington Corporation, in New York City.

Following an initial assignment as Director of Sales for the Chemicals Division, I was promoted to division General Manager, taking P&L responsibility for several key businesses including management of three foreign subsidiaries.

My team's efforts contributed to the major growth in sales, profit contribution, and return on investment of the division, recently renamed the Specialty Products Division.

As a result of the recent sale of this division, I have elected to make a career change and am writing to ask your help. A resume which details my accomplishments at Worthington Corporation, as well as my eight years at Dow Chemical, is attached.

Compensation and location are secondary to opportunity. Ideally, I'd like an assignment at either the general management or senior corporate marketing/sales management level, with an opportunity to match or better my 1997 total cash compensation of $136,000.

If my background should match any of your current or near future search assignments, I would be pleased to meet with you at your convenience. Thank you for your consideration.

Sincerely,

Florence D. Stevens

Florence G. Stevens

Attachment

ROGER A. CLARKE
722 Hummingbird Lane
Smyrna, DE 19898

July 16, 1999

Ms. Carol G. Newman
Newman & Newman Co., Ltd.
48 Helen Drive
Queensbury, NY 12804

Dear Ms. Newman:

If one of your client companies is in search of a seasoned, results-oriented senior sales executive to lead their sales and marketing function, you may want to give careful consideration to my qualifications for the position.

Review of the enclosed resume will reveal that I have over 15 years of sales management experience, with demonstrated leadership ability in directing and motivating sales organizations to consistently achieve record sales performance. In my last three positions, for example, the functions that I have managed have set new sales records each and every year, with an average increase of nearly 20% per year!

My qualifications include an M.B.A. in Marketing from the University of Connecticut and nearly 18 years in consumer product sales. For the last four years I have been Regional Sales Manager for Lever Brothers in the Northeast Region, where I have managed an 80-person sales organization that covers a ten state area.

My current compensation is $125,000, consisting of a base salary of $95,000 and bonus of $30,000. I am seeking a position at the national sales or sales/marketing level with broader accountability and the opportunity for substantial earnings improvement.

I would be pleased to meet with you to further discuss my credentials and to explore appropriate management opportunities with your clients. Thank you for your consideration, and I look forward to hearing from you.

Sincerely,

Roger A. Clarke

Roger A. Clarke

Enclosure

JANICE H. WOLFSON

255 Cedar Valley Drive
Highland Park, IL 60035

Home: (312) 633-7147
Office: (312) 593-9098

August 22, 1999

Mr. Robert M. Montgomery
R.M. Montgomery Assoc., Inc.
55 Madison Ave., Ste. 200
Morristown, NJ 07960

Dear Mr. Montgomery:

My research indicates that your firm specializes in executive search consulting in the financial field. Since I am in search of a position in financial management, I have therefore enclosed my resume for your review against the current needs of your clients.

Briefly, my credentials include an M.B.A. in Finance from the University of Vermont and ten years experience in finance with Barrington Industries, where I am now Manager of Corporate Finance. Barrington Industries, as you may know, is a $500 million manufacturer of floor coverings. In this capacity, I manage a six-person department with functional responsibility for domestic and international finance, money & banking, financial planning and analysis and treasury.

It appears that my career has peaked here at Barrington, since the current Chief Financial Officer is only two years my senior and is planning to remain with the company. I am therefore seeking a position as Chief Financial Officer with a small to medium-sized manufacturing company, where I can report to the Chief Executive Officer and assume total responsibility for the firm's financial function.

My compensation requirements are in the $100,000 to $115,000 range.

Thank you for reviewing my credentials. I look forward to hearing from you should you feel I would be a suitable candidate for one of your current or future search assignments.

Very truly yours,

Janice H. Wolfson

Janice H. Wolfson

Enclosure

WALTER C. PAGE
101 W. Eagle Road
Havertown, PA 19083
(215) 499-8032

July 15, 1999

Mr. Peter R. Hendelman
PRH Management, Inc.
2777 Summer Street
Stamford, CT 06905

Dear Mr. Hendelman:

I am advised by one of my colleagues that your firm has some specialization in conducting executive search assignments in the field of distribution management. I am pleased, therefore, to forward a copy of my resume for review against your current search assignments in this field.

My qualifications include a B.A. in Business Administration from Villanova University and 18 years experience in distribution management, most of which has been with Burlington Industries, where I am currently Corporate Manager of Warehousing and Distribution. In this capacity, I report to the Vice President of Logistics and manage a 350 employee, 12 warehouse transportation and distribution function for this $6 billion corporation.

Under my leadership, Burlington has realized over $25 million in annual cost savings during the last three years alone, as I have streamlined distribution operations and implemented far-reaching strategies aimed at productivity improvement. I am currently directing four major new initiatives that should add another $8 to $10 million annual cost savings to the bottom line over the next two years.

Perhaps one of your clients might be interested in my ability to bring similar cost savings and efficiencies to their operations. If so, I would welcome the opportunity to meet with you to explore this possibility.

I am seeking a position at the Director level in distribution management with full accountability for a company's distribution planning and operations. Compensation requirements are in the $85,000 to $100,000 range, dependent upon location and nature of the position.

Thank you for your consideration and I look forward to hearing from you should you have an appropriate opportunity to discuss with me.

Sincerely,

Walter C. Page

Walter C. Page

Enclosure

GERALD A. HELMSLEY
1722 Whitehall Avenue
Brockton, MA 02401

September 2, 1999

Mr. R. J. Wymar
Wytmar & Co., Inc.
254 Donlea Road
Barrington, IL 60010

Dear Mr. Wymar:

I understand that your company enjoys an excellent reputation as a retained executive search firm in the marketing field. Perhaps you may have an active search assignment for a senior marketing executive with my credentials.

My qualifications include an M.B.A. in Marketing from the University of Michigan and some 16 years marketing and sales experience in the specialty chemicals field. Currently Director of Marketing for the Specialty Chemicals Division of Dow Chemical Company, I manage a staff of 12 brand managers, market analysts and research support personnel in the marketing of a wide range of specialty chemicals sold to numerous industrial applications.

During my last three years in this position, we have successfully introduced over 15 products accounting for over $400 million in new sales. All but one product entry has either reached or exceeded sales expectations, with better than half the products exceeding first year goals by more than 25%.

I am now seeking a position as either vice president or director of marketing sales at the corporate level. Obviously, my strength is in the chemical or specialty chemicals field. Compensation requirements are in the $140+ range, and I will consider relocation to most areas of the country.

Should you have an appropriate search assignment that is a match for my qualifications and interests, I would welcome a call. Thank you for your consideration.

Sincerely,

Gerald A. Helmsley

Gerald A. Helmsley

Enclosure

GRACE M. OTTINGER

737 Chrysanthemum Lane, Silver Springs, MD 21339

January 16, 1999

Mr. Blake D. Edwards
The Edwards Group
909 Blue Grass Plaza, SW
Lexington, KY 57027

Dear Mr. Edwards:

As an employment agency specializing in the recruitment of engineering talent for the pulp and paper industry, you may have some interest in my background. A resume is enclosed for your reference.

Briefly, I am a mechanical engineer with strong project background in the converting of coated and fine papers. I hold a B.S. degree from the University of Maryland, and have spent the last five years as a project engineer with the Carver Paper Company at the Hastings Mill. As you are likely aware, this mill is currently for sale and future career opportunities are therefore uncertain.

I am seeking a position as a senior project engineer or engineering manager within the paper industry, with a particular interest in either papermaking or converting. Assignments in general mill engineering would not be of interest.

I am completely open to relocation, and my salary requirements are in the $65,000 to $70,000 range.

Since my employer is unaware of my decision to make a change, I ask that my candidacy be handled with appropriate discretion.

Thank you for your assistance and I look forward to hearing from you should you locate a suitable opportunity which you feel may be of interest to me.

Sincerely,

Grace M. Ottinger

Enclosure

EARL P. SHERIDAN
6 Willingham Court
Augusta, GA 30836

March 23, 1999

Mr. Marshall W. Rotella, Jr.
The Corporate Connection
7024 Glen Forest Drive
Richmond, VA 23226

Dear Mr. Rotella:

I have recently learned of your firm's specialization in executive search consulting in the field of operations management. Enclosed, therefore, please find a copy of my resume for review against current or future searches that you may be conducting on behalf of a client organization.

My qualifications include a B.S. in Mechanical Engineering from Georgia Tech, followed by an M.B.A. from M.I.T.'s Sloan School of Business. Since graduation from Sloan in 1990, I have been with the General Electric Company in manufacturing management in the company's Small Motors Division.

In the last seven years since joining G.E., I have experienced rapid advancement, starting with a position as a Manufacturing Supervisor at a small motors manufacturing facility in Rochester, New York, and culminating with my current assignment as General manager for a 1,200 employee manufacturing facility located in Batesburg, South Carolina. Details of my various assignments and specific accomplishments are highlighted on the enclosed resume.

I am seeking a senior-level manufacturing position at the director or vice president level, with full P&L responsibility for a multi-plant operation. My preference would be to remain within the electrical field, since I already have seven years invested in this industry. Compensation requirements are in the $125,000 base range plus bonus.

Should one of your clients be looking for a fast-track manufacturing executive with excellent experience and solid accomplishments in the electrical field, I would appreciate hearing from you.

Thank you for your consideration.

Sincerely,

Earl P. Sheridan

Earl P. Sheridan

Enclosure

4

Advertising Response Cover Letters

Employment advertising has long been a major source of jobs for those engaged in job hunting. Print advertising in newspapers and professional/trade journals, accounts for an estimated 10 to 14 percent of all jobs that are found.

Knowing how to respond effectively to recruitment advertising is an important element of one's job-hunting effort. How effectively one responds to such advertising has a definite bearing on whether an employment interview will follow. Poorly written letters containing improper grammar and/or lack of focus can lead to ruined employment chances. By contrast, well-written cover letters can often be a key factor in landing that all-important employment interview.

THE ADVANTAGE

The key advantage of the advertising cover letter, compared to the general broadcast letter used for mass mailing to employers and search firms, is that the letter's author knows exactly what the employer is seeking. This key point "falls on deaf ears" in far too many cases.

I have been amazed by how many job seekers ignore an employer's specific requirements, as stated in an ad, and go on to describe qualifications and experience factors that are of little or no interest to would-be employers. What a shame to be blind to such a golden opportunity!

Unfortunately, such behavior is reminiscent of the salesperson who doesn't take the time to "qualify" the buyer. The sales representative fails to query the buyer sufficiently at the beginning of the sales presentation to understand what factors are "key motivators" that will cause the customer to actually buy the product. The salesperson then drones on and on about the product's many features, but fails to cover the features that are important to the buying decision. The result is no sale.

The successful sales representative first determines what product attributes are most important to the buyer's purchasing decision. By focusing the sales presentation on these motivating factors, the representative substantially increases the probability of a sale.

BEN FRANKLIN BALANCE SHEET

A good technique to use when preparing to write an advertising response cover letter is the Ben Franklin Balance Sheet. This approach is used to qualify the buyer (the employer) and to force yourself to focus only on those candidate qualifications that are important to the employer's hiring decision.

To use this approach, simply draw a line down the center of a piece of paper. Label the left column "employer's requirements." Title the right column "my qualifications."

Now carefully review the employment advertisement line-by-line, and list each of the employer's specific requirements on the left side of your balance sheet. Prioritize these key qualification factors by the emphasis that the employer appears to place on each of them in the ad. Key terms such as "must have," "prefer," and "highly desirable" often provide strong clues about the importance the employer attaches to certain candidate qualifications. Also, the order in which these qualifications are presented in the advertisement frequently indicates their relative importance, with the most critical qualifications first and least important requirements last.

Now, from your resume, prepare a list of your qualifications that coincide with the employer's requirements. Record them on the right side of your balance sheet under the heading "my qualifications" and adjacent to the relevant employer's requirements.

This simple analysis will help you to write a very effective cover letter. The basic data are readily available and are listed in the order of their importance to the employer. You are now ready to "make the sale."

LETTER COMPONENTS

The sample advertising response cover letters found in this chapter contain certain key elements. These are:

1. Reference to advertisement.
2. Expression of interest in position.
3. Comparison of employer's requirements with personal qualifications.
4. Salary requirements statement (optional).
5. Request for response or interview.
6. Statement of appreciation.

The sample letters illustrate the different ways these elements can be effectively incorporated into an advertising response cover letter.

TWO FORMATS

The advertising response cover letter normally utilizes one of two formats: the *linear* format or the *literary* format. Review of the sample resumes provided in this chapter will reveal several approaches to the use of each.

The linear format is generally used when the author wants to emphasize that he or she has all of the key qualifications required by the employer. The writer provides a line-by-line (linear) listing of these qualifications. The linear approach highlights these qualifications and facilitates the employer's direct comparison with its own requirements. This format relates directly to the stated candidate requirements contained in the employment ad and, if well presented, should systematically lead the employer to conclude that you are well qualified for the position and are worthy of an employment interview.

The literary format, on the other hand, is most frequently used when the author does not possess all of the key qualifications stated in the advertisement. The linear format should be avoided, and the writer should use the literary (or paragraph) approach.

As with the linear format, a parallel should be drawn between the letter author's qualifications and those required by the employer. The literary approach, however, makes it far less obvious to the employer that certain of these key qualifications are missing. By contrast, the linear approach highlights this void and makes it easier for the employer to routinely "screen you out."

The Ben Franklin Balance Sheet will serve you well when choosing which format to use. This balance sheet will make it clear which of the employer's qualifications you are missing and should make it fairly obvious which of these two letter formats will best meet your needs.

The balance of this chapter contains several examples of employment advertisements along with sample cover letter responses. You will note how these letters effectively employ the comparison techniques discussed in this chapter. Careful study of these sample letters should enable you to construct highly effective cover letters that significantly enhance the probabilities of landing employment interviews.

ARLENE S. DWYER
1432 S. Wabash Street
Kokomo, IN 43621

June 24, 1999

Snack-Pack, Inc.
ATTN: Human Resources Department
P.O. Box 214909
Milwaukee, WI 53221

Dear Sir or Madam:

Your ad for a Manufacturing Cost Accountant in the June 12th issue of *The Milwaukee Examiner* interests me. I am therefore forwarding my resume for your review.

As my resume will demonstrate, I would appear to have excellent qualifications for your opening. Please consider the following:

- B.A. Accounting, University of Cincinnati, 1996

- C.P.A., May 1997

- 1 year, Auditor, Coopers & Lybrand

- 1 year, Cost Accountant, Delco Electronics, (Kokomo, IN Plant)

- Well versed in standard cost accounting practices

My salary requirements are in the high $30K range.

Should you agree that my background is a good match for your requirements, I would welcome the opportunity to meet with you personally. I can be reached on a confidential basis during the day at (317) 992-3176.

Thank you for your consideration and I look forward to hearing from you.

Sincerely,

Arlene S. Dwyer

Arlene S. Dwyer

Enclosure

CORPORATE CONTROLLER

Barrymore, Inc. is a $250 million manufacturer of quality hardwood flooring with distribution throughout the Northeastern United States. We are a 25-year-old company whose sales and profits have nearly tripled in the last 3 years alone.

The position of Corporate Controller reports to the Chief Financial Officer with responsibility for preparation of all quarterly and annual consolidated returns, S.E.C. reporting, accounts receivable, accounts payable, cost accounting, tax research & preparation, credit and audit. Reporting to this position are 4 managers and a staff of 12 professional and support personnel.

This position requires a B.S. in Accounting and at least five years corporate accounting management experience in a multi-plant, multi-state manufacturing environment. Must be thoroughly versed in preparation of consolidated statements, S.E.C. requirements and standard accounting practices. A CPA and at least two years public accounting experience also required.

Highly competitive salary and attractive executive bonus program are provided. Comprehensive benefits program also furnished. For consideration, please forward resume to:

★ BARRYMORE, INC. ★
101 Merrimac Street
Boston, MA 02114

ATTN: Daniel Ridding

EOE

1733 Blythe Avenue
Drexel Hill, PA 19026

April 30, 1998

Mr. Daniel Ridding
Barrymore, Inc.
101 Merrimac Street
Boston, MA 02114

Dear Mr. Ridding:

I am submitting my resume in response to your April 28th ad in the *Boston Globe* for a Corporate Controller. This sounds like an interesting position and I would welcome the opportunity to discuss it with you personally.

It would appear that my qualifications are an excellent match for your requirements.

In keeping with your specification, I hold a B.S. in Accounting from Widener University and have over five years corporate accounting experience with Best Liebco Corporation, a manufacturer of paint brushes. Best Liebco has six manufacturing facilities in five states.

As Manager of Corporate Accounting, I am responsible for preparation of the company's consolidated returns on both a quarterly and annual basis. I am well-trained in standard accounting procedures and thoroughly versed in S.E.C. requirements.

I completed my C.P.A. in 1988, while an Auditor with Arthur Andersen. My credentials include over three years public accounting experience.

I believe that I am exceptionally well-qualified for the position advertised, and that I could make a meaningful contribution to your company. I hope that we will have the opportunity to meet to further discuss the specifics of your requirements.

Thank you for your consideration.

Sincerely,

Deborah M. Cohen

Deborah M. Cohen

DMC/rac

Enclosure

FRANCIS J. TUCKER

617 Righter's Mill Road
Fort Edward, NY 14936

Office: (518) 876-9314
Home: (518) 775-3047

March 31, 1998

Mr. Gerald Theder
Employment Manager
Eaton Chemical Company
2388 Cole Street
Scranton, PA 17652

Dear Mr. Theder:

Your ad in the March 28th edition of *The Philadelphia Inquirer* for Sales Representatives - Specialty Chemicals caught my eye. This sounds like an exciting opportunity that is very much in keeping with my career objectives, and I would appreciate the chance to meet with you to discuss this opportunity further.

Careful review of your requirements suggests that I am well-qualified for this position. Consider the following:

- B.S. degree in Chemical Engineering

- 3 years selling specialty chemicals to the corrugated industry

- General knowledge of papermaking processes

- Strong technical problem-solving skills (used as regional resource on tough customer problems)

My interpersonal skills are solid, and I am frequently called upon to make important customer presentations due to my excellent communication and presentation skills. In addition, you might like to know that I was the leading Sales Representative in the Northeast Region in 1997.

Hopefully, you are convinced that I have the talent and motivation required to make a strong contribution to Eaton Chemical Company and we will have the opportunity to meet in the near future.

Thank you for your consideration and I look forward to hearing from you.

Very truly yours,

Francis J. Tucker

Francis J. Tucker

Enclosure

DIRECTOR
SALES & MARKETING

Barnam Sealing Systems, a leading manufacturer of high-performance sealing systems and gasket products for automotive and industrial applications is seeking a Director of Sales & Marketing to manage its corporate marketing/sales function.

This position reports to the President and is responsible for developing and leading the strategy needed to support the company's aggressive growth plans. Products are sold both direct and through distributor network to O.E.M. accounts.

We seek a degreed executive with a strong background in marketing and sales management to O.E.M. accounts. Must be a talented leader/motivator with a solid track record in continuously achieving sales objectives. Must be good strategic thinker who can contribute to the management of the business as a member of the senior management team.

If qualified and interested in this position, please send resume and salary history to:

Angela M. Murray
Executive Vice President

BARNAM SEALING SYSTEMS, INC.
3813 North Redding Road
Muncie, IN 47304-1332

Equal Opportunity Employer, M/F

PAUL C. MAGGIO

1432 Rodney Road
Buffalo, NY 14203

Home: (716) 752-0337
Office: (716) 835-6800

October 16, 1998

Ms. Angela M. Murray
Executive Vice President
Barnam Sealing Systems, Inc.
3813 North Redding Road
Muncie, IN 47304-1332

Dear Ms. Murray:

I am forwarding my resume in response to your October 15th ad in the *Indiana Star* for a Director - Sales & Marketing. This position sounds quite interesting, and I would appear to fit the candidate specifications as detailed in your ad.

Specifically, I hold an MBA in Marketing and have over ten years marketing and sales management experience selling to O.E.M. accounts. As Director of Marketing for Fuel Jet Carburetors, I manage a 30 employee marketing and field sales organization selling automotive carburetors to car and truck engine manufacturers through both a distributor network and direct.

During the last five years in this capacity, my marketing and sales strategies have led to a 250% increase in sales volume coupled with a profit increase of nearly 300%. I am known for being a key contributor to the business planning process and am credited with revitalizing and motivating the marketing and sales organization through creative leadership.

I would welcome the opportunity to meet with you to explore how I might bring added value to Barnam Sealing Systems' marketing and sales effort through solid strategic planning and effective managerial leadership.

My current compensation is $125,000 ($100,000 base salary plus $25,000 bonus). I also have a company furnished automobile and other minor executive perks.

Thank you for your consideration and I look forward to hearing from you.

Sincerely,

Paul C. Maggio

Paul C. Maggio

PCM:rms

Enclosure

FINANCIAL ANALYST

Fortune 200 consumer products company seeks Financial Analyst for Corporate Planning Group.

Position reports to the Manager of Strategic Planning and will participate in the evaluation of various strategic business options including: acquisitions & mergers, new business development, and expansion/consolidation of existing businesses. Will regularly interface with senior executive officers, including the presentation of study findings and recommendations regarding alternate business strategies.

Successful candidate will hold an MBA from a highly quantitative business school with emphasis in Finance. Must have excellent interpersonal and communications skills, including the presence and poise needed to interface effectively with executive level management. Some prior experience in merger and acquisition analysis helpful.

Please forward resume and salary requirements to:

Ms. Carla A. Bullock
Administrative Employment Manager

American Home Products, Inc.
685 Third Avenue
New York, NY 10017-6047

Equal Opportunity Employer, M/F

DIANE M. SANTORO

747 Copperfield Avenue
Wilmington, DE 19898

Home: (302) 621-0973
Office: (302) 433-2076

February 22, 1998

Ms. Carla A. Bullock
Administrative Employment Manager
American Home Products, Inc.
685 Third Avenue
New York, NY 10017-6047

Dear Ms. Bullock:

I noted your ad for a Financial Analyst in this Sunday's edition of the *Delaware Star Ledger* with a great deal of interest. Your candidate description appears to be an excellent match with my personal profile.

Please consider the following:

- MBA, St. Joseph's University, Honors Graduate (Finance Major)

- Excellent communication skills:
    - Debate Team President, 1996 and 1997
    - Actress, four plays
    - English 101 (Freshman Composition), Grade = A

- Evidence of Interpersonal/Leadership Skills
    - Sorority President, two years
    - Sorority Vice President, one year

My extracurricular activities and summer work experience have enabled me to develop the poise and maturity needed to effectively relate to senior-level management. Additionally, I assisted in merger and acquisition analysis during my summer employment with the DuPont Company.

I believe that these qualifications, along with my drive and enthusiasm, would make me an excellent candidate for your opening. I would hope to have the opportunity to meet with you during a visit to American Home Products.

Thank you for your consideration.

Very truly yours,

Diane M. Santoro

Diane M. Santoro

Enclosure

VICE PRESIDENT
FINANCE

We are a $250 million manufacturer of electronic components for the defense industry. A large federal contract has necessitated that we double our size in the next 18 months, requiring total restructuring of our finances.

This position reports to the Chief Financial Officer with full responsibility for day-to-day direction of the company's financial functions including money & banking, domestic finance, international finance and credit.

We seek a seasoned financial manager with a minimum of 10 years experience in the defense manufacturing industry. Must be thoroughly versed in financial theory and highly innovative in the approaches to raising capital and restructuring corporate debt load.

Excellent interpersonal, communications and managerial skills required.

Send resume and compensation requirements to:

Box 1301
WASHINGTON POST
1150 15th Street, NW
Washington, DC 20071

ROBERT C. MOORE
36 Westgate Circle
Villanova, PA 19057

October 26, 1998

Box 1301
Washington Post
1150 15th Street, NW
Washington, DC 20071

Dear Sir or Madam:

I am interested in talking with you concerning your need for a Vice President of Finance as described in your October 26th ad in the *Washington Post*. This appears to be an exciting opportunity and I appear to have the profile that you are seeking.

My resume is enclosed for your review and consideration.

As specified in your advertisement, I am a seasoned financial manager with over ten years experience in the defense manufacturing industry. Specifically, I am Manager of Corporate Finance with JetStar Electronics, a supplier of weaponry guidance systems for military vehicles.

My credentials include an MBA in Finance from the University of Chicago, and I am well-schooled in financial theory and its applications.

As evidence of my innovation, despite loss of its AA financial rating and an after-tax loss of $20 million in 1996, I was able to secure a $130 million line of credit at prime rate for JetStar. By restructuring the corporate debt load and providing the funding for a $100 million capital expansion program, JetStar was able to "turn the corner" and return to profitability.

Our 1997 after-tax profit was $22 million, a healthy 16% ROI! Additionally, our AA financial rating has been restored and JetStar is now on the "recommended buy" list of several of the nation's leading brokerage houses.

Perhaps I could make a similar contribution to your company. I would welcome the opportunity to explore this possibility during a personal interview.

I appreciate your consideration and look forward to hearing from you. Thank you.

Sincerely,

Robert C. Moore

Robert C. Moore

Enclosure

MARKETING BRAND MANAGER
CONSUMER PRODUCTS

Fortune 200 consumer products company with annual sales of $6.2 billion seeks Marketing Brand Manager for leading hair care product line. Need bright, innovative individual who can revitalize sagging sales and restore product to its dominant market position.

Position requires an MBA in Marketing and 5+ years marketing experience in consumer products industry. Must have demonstrated brand management skills and proven record of significant marketing contribution as measured by sales volume and market share.

Successful candidate will be highly creative, resourceful and possess excellent interpersonal and communications skills. Business team leadership and an appreciation for the participative style of management should be well-evidenced.

Excellent base salary plus participation in management incentive plan are offered, plus a highly competitive benefits package.

For consideration, forward resume in confidence to:

Manager of Professional Employment

BRECKENRIDGE LABORATORIES
10525 Waveland Avenue
Bloomfield Hills, MI 48302-0947

Equal Opportunity Employer, M/F

CLAUDIA S. BARD

167 Chadwick Commons, Los Angeles, CA 90334

June 26, 1998

Manager of Professional Employment
Breckenridge Laboratories
10525 Waveland Avenue
Bloomfield Hills, MI 48302-0947

Dear Sir/Madam:

You sparked my interest with your ad for a Marketing Brand Manager - Consumer Products in today's *Los Angeles Times*. This sounds like an exciting opportunity, and I would appear to have the qualifications you are seeking.

Please consider my credentials:

- MBA in Marketing, Stanford University, 1993

- 5 years Consumer Marketing Experience (The Gillette Company, Corporate Marketing Department)

- Brand management marketing results include:

    - 20 point market share increase, *Foamy-For-Her* Shaving Cream
    - 50% sales increase, *Chic* Disposable Razors
    - 14 point market share increase, *Buff-Away* Exfoliating Cleanser

I am noted for being an effective communicator and an excellent team player. I frequently serve as facilitator during business team meetings, and am skilled at maximizing group participation and creating a feeling of "team ownership" around marketing plans and strategies. I am a strong advocate of the "participative" style of management and enjoy excellent interpersonal relationships with others.

Should you have an interest in me, I would be pleased to visit Breckenridge Laboratories to further explore this opportunity with you and the members of your Marketing Staff.

Thank you for your consideration, and I look forward to hearing from you in the near future.

Sincerely,

Claudia S. Bard

Claudia S. Bard

Enclosure

PHILIP A. THORNTON
270 Blair Mill Road
Deerfield, IL 60336

September 22, 1998

Ms. Virginia Templeton
Vice President Marketing
Microfiche Systems International
423 York Street
Springfield, OH 45505

Dear Ms. Templeton:

Your September 21st ad in the *Illinois Post* for a Director of Marketing has stimulated considerable interest on my part. I am therefore submitting my resume for your review and consideration.

Much of my background closely parallels your specific requirements, and I would appear to be well-qualified for this opportunity.

I hold an MBA in Marketing and am currently Manager of Marketing for SAP, a $300 million manufacturer of computer systems and software sold primarily to banks, insurance companies and government agencies. I am familiar with the financial record keeping requirements of these organizations.

Under my marketing leadership, SAP has more than doubled its annual sales in the last five years. This growth has been driven by the highly successful introduction of two new product lines -- SAP System IV and System V. Additionally, System I has been successfully repositioned in the market, resulting in a 15% gain in market share.

My knowledge of your target markets, coupled with demonstrated success in the marketing of major new system products, strongly suggests that I could make a significant contribution to your marketing and business objectives. Perhaps we could meet to more thoroughly explore this possibility.

My compensation requirements are in the low six figure range.

I appreciate your consideration, and look forward to the possibility of meeting with you and the members of your senior management team. Thank you.

Sincerely,

Phillip A. Thornton

Philip A. Thornton

Enclosure

PROJECT ENGINEER

Craftsman, Inc., the world's leader in the manufacture and sale of power tools, seeks Project Engineer for its 1,000 employee manufacturing facility in New Haven. This is an excellent opportunity for fresh graduate looking for first exposure to plant project engineering.

Position reports to Senior Project Engineer and is responsible for assisting in the engineering, installation and start-up of small tool manufacturing equipment.

Ideal candidate will have B.S. in Mechanical Engineering and a strong desire for hands-on project work. Above average academic performance and/or demonstrated leadership potential highly desirable.

Excellent compensation and complete benefits program provided.

Interested candidates should send resume to:

Mr. Ben Johnson
Technical Employment Manager

CRAFTSMAN, INC.
30 Bernard Road
New Haven, CT 06473

Equal Opportunity Employer

LUCILLE B. CHEN

2401 Welsh Hall, #414
College Station, Texas 77845

_____

February 22, 1998

Mr. Ben Johnson
Technical Employment Manager
Craftsman, Inc.
30 Bernard Road
New Haven, CT 06473

Dear Mr. Johnson:

The position of Project Engineer which you advertised in this Sunday's edition of the _Houston Chronicle_ sounds like the kind of job for which I am looking. Additionally, I would seem to be an excellent match for your requirements.

My qualifications include:

- B.S. in Mechanical Engineering, Texas A&M

- Grade Point Average = 3.4/4.0

- Demonstrated leadership includes:
  - Captain, Varsity Swim Team, 1998
  - Vice President, KD Sorority, 1997
  - Vice President, A.S.M.E., 1997

I have always preferred hands-on as opposed to theoretical work. This is clearly demonstrated through several of my hobbies: auto repair/maintenance, furniture refinishing, construction and remodeling, etc.

Additionally, my co-op assignment as Assistant Plant Project Engineer at Welbilt Corporation has provided me with practical, hands-on plant project engineering experience.

May I have the opportunity to meet with you and the members of your Plant Engineering Staff?

I look forward to hearing from you.

Sincerely,

Lucille B. Chen

Lucille B. Chen

Enclosure

DIRECTOR OF ENGINEERING

Major manufacturer of coated papers seeks executive to head its 150-employee central engineering group.

Position reports to Vice President of Technology and is responsible, through engineering staff, for directing all capital project work, including mill construction, expansions and major rebuild projects. Will manage annual capital projects budget of $400 to $600 million.

Seek seasoned engineering executive with 20+ years experience in the paper industry. Must demonstrate ability to effectively direct and manage sizeable engineering department with large scale, multiple project workload. Must be a strong advocate/practitioner of participative management and believe in the importance of "employee stakeholders" as the key to employee morale and productivity.

Highly competitive base salary plus executive bonus plan. Excellent range of cafeteria-style benefits also available.

For consideration, please forward complete resume and compensation requirements to:

Ms. Susan Sciscione
Director of Employment

Ⓠ CONSOLIDATED PAPER, INC.
Box 1607
Ann Arbor, MI 48231

4710 Summer Lane
Appleton, WI 55703

August 15, 1998

Ms. Susan Sciscione
Director of Employment
Consolidated Paper, Inc.
Box 1607
Ann Arbor, MI 48231

Dear Ms. Sciscione:

I am forwarding my resume in response to your August 15th ad in the <u>Wisconsin Herald</u> for the position of Director of Engineering. This appears to be an exciting opportunity and one for which I am well-qualified.

As called for in your advertisement, I am a seasoned engineering executive with over 20 years experience in the paper industry. In my current position as Manager of Corporate Engineering for Appleton Paper Company, I direct a 40 employee central engineering group accountable for all capital project work (new equipment installation and rebuilds) at four paper manufacturing/converting mills. Our annual capital budget is in the $300 to $500 million range.

Some major capital projects which I have directed include:

- Engineering & Construction of Neenah Mill
  (40 TPD Corrugated Plant; Capital budget: $350 million)

- Complete Rebuild of two fine paper machines
  (Madison, WI Plant; Capital Expense: $210 million)

I am both a strong advocate and practitioner of the "participative" approach to management. I endeavor to involve my subordinates in all aspects of department operations, from strategic planning through day-to-day operations. I have personally led and facilitated several productivity task forces, which have included representation from all levels of the engineering organization. I recognize the value of the "employee stakeholder" concept.

I feel I have the qualifications to make a strong contribution to Consolidated Paper's Central Engineering Group and hope that you agree. I would welcome the opportunity to meet with you. My compensation requirements are in the low $100K range.

I look forward to hearing from you shortly. Thank you.

Sincerely,

Michael C. O'Brien

Michael C. O'Brien

Enclosure

ADMINISTRATIVE RECRUITER

We seek an experienced recruiter to handle all administrative employment for our $200 million, multi-plant baked goods manufacturing company.

Position reports to the Director of Human Resources and is responsible for the recruitment and hiring of all administrative, marketing and sales professionals.

Successful candidate will have a college degree coupled with 1-2 years experience in a corporate employment function. Should be knowledgeable concerning the cost effective use of employment sources, including college recruiting.

If interested, please forward your resume to:

Mr. Daniel R. Boyle
Director of Human Resources

The Tasty Baking Company
1010 S. Front Street
Philadelphia, PA 19101

Equal Opportunity Employer, M/F

MARGARET T. JANSON

476 Westover Lane
Jacksonville, FL 33923

Home: (813) 255-3241
Office: (813) 992-6706

January 12, 1998

Mr. Daniel R. Boyle
Director of Human Resources
The Tasty Baking Company
1010 S. Front Street
Philadelphia, PA 19101

Dear Mr. Boyle:

I noted your ad for an Administrative Recruiter in the Sunday edition of *The Philadelphia Inquirer* with a great deal of interest. I am planning a move to the Philadelphia area and would seem to be exceptionally well-qualified for the position you advertised.

I hold a B.A. degree in English from Dickinson College and have spent the last three years as Employment Manager for Stuckey's Candies, where I have been heavily involved in the successful recruitment of all administrative personnel.

My current assignment requires that I deal effectively with a wide range of recruitment sources. These have included: college recruiting, employment advertising, employee referral systems, resume databases, alumni associations, professional and trade associations, etc.

In the three years that I have been in this position, I have reduced agency fees by 80% (annual savings of $330,000) and reduced the interview-to-hire ratio from 8:1 to 2.5:1. This improved ratio has saved considerable managerial time and returned an estimated $85,000 per year to candidate travel expense.

I am well-motivated to continuously bring improvement to the employment process and to reduce employment costs.

May I have the opportunity of meeting with you during my forthcoming trip to Philadelphia? I will be in your area from February 6th through the 20th.

Thank you for your consideration, and I look forward to hearing from you shortly.

Sincerely,

Margaret T. Janson

Margaret T. Janson

Enclosure

SENIOR VICE PRESIDENT
HUMAN RESOURCES

Internationally-known 12-plant, 12,000 employee specialty glass manufacturer seeks top Human Resources officer for corporate staff.

Position reports to the President, and is accountable for management of 28-employee staff. Functional responsibilities include organization design, staffing, training & development, compensation & benefits, employee & labor relations, diversity and safety & hygiene.

Our client seeks a seasoned Human Resources professional with 15+ years experience, including management of a sizeable HR staff operation. Requires a Master's degree in Human Resources or Psychology with strengths in organization design and development and labor relations.

Must be a strategic leader capable of orchestrating and leading major cultural change efforts aimed at substantially improving the use and productivity of human assets. Must also be a strong advocate of the participative management philosophy and be capable of providing strategic leadership in the corporate-wide transition from "top down" management to "employee empowered" processes.

Interested candidates, please forward resumes and salary requirements to:

Ms. Nona Robinson

Mellon-Briggs, Inc.
Executive Search Consultants
2324 Concord Highway
Monroe, NC 28110

SHELIA C. RHOADS

290 Plumstead Avenue
Charlotte, NC 28217

Home: (704) 249-8730
Office: (704) 357-1000

April 23, 1998

Ms. Nona Robinson
Mellon-Briggs, Inc.
Executive Search Consultants
2324 Concord Highway
Monroe, NC 28110

Dear Ms. Robinson:

I was intrigued by your ad in today's edition of *The Charlotte Observer* and am enclosing my resume for your consideration. It seems that I have some excellent qualifications for this position and that my background should be of strong interest to your client.

I am a heavily seasoned Human Resources professional with an M.S. degree in Psychology and over 15 years experience. In my current position as Director of Human Resources for Wellman Corporation, I manage a staff of 35 and provide a full range of Human Resource services to the corporate staff and eight manufacturing plants.

In my earlier assignment as Director of Organization Development, I was heavily involved in organization design and development activities. This included a major redesign and restructuring of the corporate staff. I was also instrumental, as a Senior O.D. Consultant, in successfully leading and facilitating a major shift in organization culture from a traditional management system to one that is based on socio-technical concepts.

I have always made a point of staying current with new, evolving Human Resource concepts, and am quick to seize the opportunity to introduce those having positive effect on productivity. I value being a strong strategic contributor and am known for my innovativeness.

My salary requirements are in the low $100K range.

May I have the pleasure of meeting with you to discuss your client's requirements in greater detail? I believe this would prove a mutually beneficial meeting.

I appreciate your consideration and look forward to hearing from you.

Sincerely,

Shelia C. Rhoads

Shelia C. Rhoads

Enclosure

PRODUCT DEVELOPMENT
ENGINEER

Leading manufacturer of nonwoven materials seeks Product Development Engineer for R&D Group.

Position reports to Product Development Group Leader in the development of new, air-layed materials to be used as inner and outer barriers for disposable diaper liners and similar proprietary applications.

Requirements include an advanced degree in Chemical Engineering, Materials Science or Polymer Chemistry with 2-3 years research experience in nonwovens product development. Strong knowledge of polymer chemistry and fiber structures a must. Exposure to super absorbent materials technology a definite plus.

Please forward resume along with salary requirements to:

Dr. Timothy L. Lim
Director of Administrative Services
Technology Group

FIBERTECH, INC.
1515 Church Street
Princeton, NJ 08969

Equal Opportunity Employer, M/F

JAY R. FELLER

188 Smithbridge Road
New Brunswick, NJ 08799

Home: (201) 922-6728
Office: (201) 454-1306

August 22, 1998

Dr. Timothy L. Lim
Director of Administrative Services
Technology Group
Fibertech, Inc.
1515 Church Street
Princeton, NJ 08969

Dear Dr. Lim:

I was delighted to see your recent advertisement for a Product Development Engineer in the July issue of *Pulp & Paper Research Newsletter*. It seems that my qualifications and interests are a close match for your requirements. I am equally delighted that the position is local and would not require my relocation.

Interestingly, I am currently working as a Research Scientist for the Paper Chemicals Division of ICI Americas, a major supplier of polymers to the nonwovens industry. My principal accountability is the development of novel, new polymer materials for various nonwovens applications, including super-absorbency. I am thoroughly versed in polymer science and have expert knowledge of fibrous structures (especially nonwoven structures).

I hold a Ph.D. in Chemical Engineering from the University of Michigan and have been awarded 16 U.S. patents having to do with polymeric materials and fibrous structures. Ten of these are in the nonwovens field.

I trust that my qualifications will be of interest to you, and that we may have the opportunity to meet for the purpose of discussing your requirements in greater detail.

My salary requirements are in the mid $70K range, however, I am flexible dependent upon the specifics of the opportunity.

Thank you for your consideration, and I hope to hear from you shortly.

Very truly yours,

Jay R. Feller

Jay R. Feller

Enclosure

DIRECTOR
PROCESS DEVELOPMENT

We are a Fortune 200, sanitary tissue, personal care and cleaning products company with sales in the $5 billion range. The world leader in the manufacture of towels and tissues, our company has maintained its competitive edge through its commitment to continuous research and development.

We are in need of a Director of Process Development to lead our research efforts in the area of wet-lay sheet formation process development. This position reports to the Vice President of Technology and is responsible for leading a 15-person department in the development of new paper making processes, from bench scale through pilot plant studies.

Position requires a Ph.D. in Chemical Engineering, Chemistry, or other relevant technical discipline, and a minimum of 10 years research in paper making process development. Must be thoroughly knowledgeable in the application of twin-wire sheet forming technology and have led successful development programs in the development of novel paper making processes.

Excellent interpersonal, communications and leadership skills are also a requirement.

Please forward complete resume, along with compensation requirements, to:

Mr. Sean J. Carson
Employment Manager · Technology

HANSON PAPER COMPANY
450 Belmont Street
Paoli, PA 19430

Equal Opportunity Employer, M/F

PAUL E. KINGSLEY, Ph.D.

716 Rampart Way, Neenah, WI 53302

November 20, 1998

Mr. Sean J. Carson
Employment Manager - Technology
Hanson Paper Company
450 Belmont Street
Paoli, PA 19430

Dear Mr. Carson:

Your ad for a Director of Process Development in the November issue of the *TAPPI Journal* seems a surprisingly good match for my background. I have a strong interest in the position and am therefore submitting my resume for your consideration.

The following listing of qualifications highlights the closeness of this match:

- Ph.D. in Chemical Engineering

- Twelve (12) years papermaking process development (tissue and towel products)

- Expert in twin-wire sheet formation (8 patents)

- Principal Scientist in development of revolutionary new transpiration drying process

- Research group leader to highly successful wet lay tissue development process (5 patents)

In my current position as Process Development Group Leader, I have been a successful advocate of several new technology concepts, providing solid evidence of both my leadership and communications skills. My ability to relate to others across the organization has frequently been cited as a key strength.

I would appreciate the opportunity to meet with you and the other members of your Technology Staff to explore how my capabilities might be used to further enhance Hanson Paper Company's competitive position in the marketplace.

My compensation requirements are in the low $90K range.

Thank you for reviewing my credentials. I look forward to hearing from you.

Sincerely,

Paul E. Kingsley

Paul E. Kingsley

Enclosure

SYSTEMS ANALYST

Medium-sized manufacturer of specialty and alloy metals seeks Systems Analyst to provide support and technical assistance in the selection, installation and start-up of new general ledger accounting system.

Ideal candidate will have a B.S. degree in Computer Science and 1-2 years experience as a Systems Analyst working on accounting computer systems. Some familiarization with general ledger accounting systems helpful, but not required. Must have sufficient project leadership experience to take the lead role in the selection and application of a major business system.

Interested parties should forward their resumes to:

Ms. Genevieve Russell
Director of Human Resources

PRIME-ALLOY, INC.
200 North 59th Street
Akron, OH 59733

Equal Opportunity Employer, M/F

HENRY D. MUELLER

122 Beakins Lane
Cincinnati, OH 45292
(513) 762-3177

August 27, 1998

Ms. Genevieve Russell
Director of Human Resources
Prime-Alloy, Inc.
200 North 59th Street
Akron, OH 59733

Dear Ms. Russell:

I am forwarding my resume in response to your August 26th ad in the *Cincinnati Enquirer* for a Systems Analyst. Comparison of my qualifications with your requirements, as specified in this advertisement, suggests that I would be an excellent candidate for this position.

Highlights of my qualifications are:

- B.S. Degree, Computer Science, Syracuse University

- 2 Years Experience, Systems Analyst

- Good knowledge of General Ledger Accounting Systems (Accounting Minor at Syracuse)

- Group Leader for Order Tracking System (A $1.5 Million Systems Project)

My qualifications suggest that I should be able to make an immediate and significant contribution to Prime-Alloy in its evaluation, selection and successful installation of a general ledger accounting system. Should you agree, I would welcome the opportunity to further explore this opportunity.

Thank you for your consideration and I look forward to hearing from you.

Very truly yours,

Henry D. Mueller

HDM/kaw

Enclosure

MANAGER OF MIS

We are a major life and casualty insurance company with assets exceeding $12 billion. We are in search of a manager for our Corporate MIS function, located in Buffalo, New York.

The Manager will report to the Vice President of Corporate Information Services and will have day-to-day accountability for all MIS operations. This includes computer operations, new systems development, systems applications, client programming and support services. Reporting to this position are four functional mangers and an 80 employee support staff.

This position requires a B.S. in Computer Science with a minimum of 12 to 15 years MIS experience with an insurance company, bank or other financial institution. Must have successfully managed a sizeable corporate MIS group and be intimately familiar with all aspects of providing a high level of systems support to a demanding client base in a fast-paced business environment.

Excellent compensation and fringe benefits package is available. Relocation assistance is provided.

Qualified individuals should send resume and salary requirements to:

Mr. Ronald C. Young
Manager of Corporate Employment

FIDELITY INSURANCE COMPANY, INC.
4055 Monticello Avenue
Augusta, GA 30836

Equal Opportunity Employer, M/F

1103 Seven Oaks Drive
Waynesboro, GA 30838

October 15, 1998

Mr. Ronald C. Young
Manager of Corporate Employment
Fidelity Insurance Company, Inc.
4055 Monticello Avenue
Augusta, GA 30836

Dear Mr. Young:

I read your October 14th ad in the *Atlanta News Journal* for a Manager of MIS with a great deal of interest. From your description, this position seems a good match for my skills and capabilities. I have enclosed my resume for your review and evaluation.

According to this advertisement, you are seeking someone with a degree in Computer Science and a minimum of 12 to 15 years MIS experience with an insurance company, bank or other financial institution. I graduated with a B.S. in Computer Science from Ohio State and have over 15 years MIS experience in the insurance industry.

Further, you state that you are seeking a candidate who has successfully managed a sizeable corporate MIS group and is intimately familiar with all aspects of providing a high level of systems support to a demanding client base in a fast-paced business environment.

As Manager of MIS for Equitable Insurance Company, I direct an 80 employee corporate MIS function providing a full range of systems support to the corporate staff and 125 branch office locations. Our clients are demanding and insist on a high level of support, despite a fast-changing business culture.

Since I am already living in Waynesboro, the position would not require relocation.

Please review my accomplishments as highlighted on the enclosed resume. Should you agree that I am well-qualified for this position, I would look forward to the opportunity of meeting with you personally to further explore my credentials and your specific requirements.

I can be reached at my office on a confidential basis during the day or at my home in the evening. Thank you for your consideration.

Sincerely,

James A. Larkin

James A. Larkin

Enclosure

CHEMICALS BUYER

We are a leader in the manufacture and sale of specialty polyurethane foams. Principal customers include the automotive and defense industries.

We seek a Chemicals Buyer to work in the Purchasing Department at our corporate offices in Los Angeles, California. This position is responsible for the bulk purchase and delivery of raw material chemicals including resins, TDI, dyes, etc.

Position requires a degreed buyer with two or more years experience in chemical purchasing. Must have successfully negotiated large bulk contracts for multi-site manufacturing operations. Should be skilled in the negotiation of long-term contracts at extremely favorable terms.

For consideration, please forward your resume and compensation requirements to:

Ms. Melinda Glavin
Director of Materials & Logistics

Foam-Ex Corporation
31162 Coastal Highway, Bldg. 22
Los Angeles, CA 94766

Equal Opportunity Employer, M/F

OWEN J. LARRABEE
610 Horeshoe Trail
Colorado Springs, CO 80944
(719) 473-2309

July 22, 1998

Ms. Melinda Glavin
Director of Materials & Logistics
Foam-Ex Corporation
31162 Coastal Highway, Bldg. 22
Los Angeles, CA 94766

Dear Ms. Glavin:

I would appear to be an excellent candidate for the position of Chemicals Buyer, as advertised by Foam-Ex in the July 12th edition of the *Denver Post*. Please accept the enclosed resume as an indication of my strong interest in this position.

Comparison of my qualifications with your requirements suggests to me that there is a solid basis for further discussion of this opportunity through a face-to-face interview. Please consider the following highlights from my background:

- B.S. degree, Chemistry Major, Penn State University

- Four years chemical purchasing experience

- Successful negotiation of multi-million dollar contracts for six plant sites

- Excellent reputation as skillful negotiator of long-term contracts at below-market rates.

My current annual compensation is $59,000 and I would anticipate an increase in the 10% range to warrant a career move at this time.

I would appreciate the opportunity to further discuss this opportunity with you and to mutually explore the contributions I might make to your purchasing function.

Thank you for your consideration and I look forward to hearing from you.

Very truly yours,

Owen J Larrabee

Owen J. Larrabee

Enclosure

JOHN D. SARBELLO

617 N. Highland Avenue   Home: (817) 523-7196
Irving, TX 76134   Office: (817) 293-0450

January 21, 1999

Ms. Vanessa Pearce
Senior Vice President, Human Resources
Paulson Foods
5 Canal Street
Garland, TX 75209

Dear Ms. Pearce:

As specified in Sunday's ad in the *Dallas Morning News,* you are searching for a Vice President - Logistics Management. I think that review of the enclosed resume could well establish that I am the candidate for this position.

Please consider the following highlights of my background:

- Seasoned Logistics Executive with 22 years experience

- Director of Logistics, Giant Foods Corporation (A $2 billion food and beverage company)

- Managed staff of 60 employees in the day-to-day operation of the corporate logistics function

- Directed the selection and successful installation of a corporate-wide order entry/ production scheduling/inventory management computer system ($2 million project)

Over the last five years, I have returned more than $8 million to the business through the application of innovative cost-savings programs aimed at improving overall logistics efficiencies. Perhaps I could make a similar contribution to Paulson Foods.

If my background is of interest, I would welcome the opportunity to meet with you and other appropriate members of your senior management team.

Thank you for considering my credentials, and I look forward to hearing from you in the near future.

Sincerely,

John D Sarbello

John D. Sarbello

Enclosure

HOWARD D. REYNOLDS

439 Longacre Lane   Home: (717) 227-1862
Harrisburg, PA 17436   Office: (717) 557-1633

June 25, 1997

Human Resources Manager
Diamond Electronics, Inc.
1600 Executive Pavilion
Ridgefield, CT 06898

Dear Sir/Madam:

Enclosed please find my resume in response to your recent advertisement in the June 24th edition of the *Philadelphia Inquirer* for a Public Affairs Associate. This position sounds exciting and I would welcome the opportunity to discuss it further with you.

As my resume will attest, I appear to have excellent qualifications for this position:

- B.A. degree, Public Affairs, University of Virginia

- Two years as Administrative Aid to U.S. Senator Richard Schultz (Considerable public contact requiring poise, maturity and strong communication skills)

- Seasoned, skilled goodwill ambassador in building and maintaining positive public image on wide range of issues

I feel that I have the knowledge, skills and motivation needed to provide strong support to your Manager of Public Affairs in effectively handling both public affairs and legislative affairs matters. My experience in government should also prove a strong asset to this position.

Should you agree that my background is a good match for your requirements, I would welcome the opportunity to meet with you to further explore this excellent opportunity. My salary requirements are in the high $40K range.

Please call me on a confidential basis at my office during the day, or at my home in the evening.

I hope that you will view my qualifications favorably and that I will be hearing from you shortly. Thank you.

Sincerely,

Howard D. Reynolds

Howard D. Reynolds

Enclosure

COMMUNICATIONS MANAGER

Public Affairs Department of large commercial bank (52 branch offices) seeks communications professional to manage employee publications and internal employee communications program. Will report to the Director of Public Affairs.

We seek degreed professional with five or more years management experience in internal communications. Must be skilled in the publication of employee newsletters as well as multi-media used for effective internal communications. Strong interpersonal and communications skills are an absolute requirement.

Qualified candidates please forward complete resume to:

Employment Manager
CONSTITUTION FEDERAL SAVINGS BANK
1000 Corporate Plaza, West
New York, NY 10101

Equal Opportunity Employer, M/F

NATALIE M. SELLINGER

125 Phillips Avenue	Home: (410) 461-3976
Baltimore, MD 21201	Office: (410) 641-6600

July 14, 1998

Employment Manager
Constitution Federal Savings Bank
1000 Corporate Plaza, West
New York, NY 10101

Dear Sir/Madam:

The position of Communications Manager, as advertised in this past Sunday's edition of the *Baltimore Sun*, sounds like an exciting opportunity. Please consider the enclosed resume an indication of my strong interest in this position.

It appears that my qualifications are an excellent match for your requirements.

Your advertisement calls for a degreed professional with five or more years management experience in internal communications. My B.A. degree in English and current position as Corporate Communications Manager for Worldwide Insurance Company should meet your expectations.

Further, your ad states that you desire someone who is skilled in the publication of employee newsletters as well as multi-media used for effective communications. I now manage the publication of a corporate monthly employee newsletter and three regional employee publications as well. My use of multi-media for internal communications covers the gamut: print media, overhead and rear screen projection, computer generated slides, audio and video cassettes, closed circuit TV, satellite transmission, etc.

Both my interpersonal and communications skills are excellent and have always been a major area of strength for me.

Your opening sounds very interesting, and I would welcome the opportunity to learn more during a personal interview at your offices. I hope that you will view my candidacy favorably, and that I might have the opportunity to further explore your requirements.

Thank you for your consideration, and I will look forward to hearing from you.

Sincerely,

Natalie M. Sellinger

Natalie M. Sellinger

Enclosure

CORPORATE PLANNING ANALYST

A key member of the Corporate Planning Team, the Corporate Planning Analyst will support the Vice President of Planning and members of the Company's senior management team in the identification, evaluation and selection of appropriate business strategies for maximizing short-term profits and long-term growth.

We seek an MBA with strong quantitative and analytical skills who thrives on financial "what if" analysis of business alternatives. In addition to analytical skills, the successful candidate will be capable of identifying/defining viable options that maximize profit potential of the firm. Exceptional communication and strong interpersonal skills are a must.

Our client is a Blue Chip leader in the petrochemical industry and offers outstanding opportunities for growth into general management.

For consideration, submit complete resume and salary requirements in strictest confidence to:

Mr. Raymond Beers
Vice President

Career Consultants, Inc.
550 Seminole Avenue
Lexington, KY 53432

Executive Search Consultants

GLENN R. STACKHOUSE

505 Plymouth Lane
Elgin, IL 60621

August 23, 1998

Mr. Raymond Beers
Vice President
Career Consultants, Inc.
550 Seminole Avenue
Lexington, KY 53432

Dear Mr. Beers:

While browsing through the <u>Chicago Tribune</u> this past Sunday, I came across your advertisement for a corporate Planning Analyst. Although I am not actively "on the market," this position appears quite interesting and has prompted me to forward my resume for your review and consideration.

Review of your client's requirements, as specified in this advertisement, seems to suggest that I should be a very viable candidate for this opportunity. Please consider the following:

-   MBA, Wharton School, University of Pennsylvania

-   Three years as Business Analyst, General Foods Corporation

-   Undergraduate Degree in Statistics with an Economics Minor

-   Performed numerous studies and made best recommendations on various business strategies (e.g., buy, sell, merge, expand, contract, diversify, specialize, etc.)

My creativity and resourcefulness in identifying and presenting alternate business options has won the confidence and trust of the senior management team, and I am frequently chosen as the Lead Analyst on major project assignments. Interpersonal and communications skills are two of my major assets.

If you agree that I am well-qualified for this important position with your client, I would welcome the chance to meet with you to further explore this opportunity. Since this is a confidential inquiry, I would much prefer being contacted at my home in the evening rather than at my office.

I appreciate your consideration, and look forward to hearing from you at your convenience. Thank you.

Sincerely,

Glenn R. Stackhouse

Glenn R. Stackhouse

Enclosure

CORPORATE PLANNING MANAGER

A Fortune 500, internationally-known fast-food company with annual sales of $7.2 billion, we are in search of a top-flight manager for our Corporate Planning function.

This position reports to the Chief Financial Officer, and manages a staff of 20 high-powered analysts. Works directly with members of the Executive Committee in the development of viable business plans and strategies designed to maximize use of corporate resources and ROI.

We seek a financial MBA with 10+ years business planning experience in a consumer products or process industry company. Must have successfully managed a team of business analysts and demonstrated the ability to formulate highly successful business strategies as measured in terms of financial results.

For consideration, please direct your complete resume with compensation requirements to:

Director of Corporate Employment

DRUMSTIX, INC.
1700 Oak Ridge Highway
Nashville, TN 64706

Equal Opportunity Employeer

MARIANNE P. BUTLER

416 Union Avenue, Nashville, TN 37202

March 12, 1997

Director of Corporate Employment
Drumstix, Inc.
1700 Oak Ridge Highway
Nashville, TN 64706

Dear Sir or Madam:

I noted your ad for a Corporate Planning Manager in the March 11th edition of *The Tennessean* with considerable interest. This sounds like an excellent opportunity, and I would appear to have the qualifications you seek. Enclosed is my resume for your consideration.

I am a Financial MBA with over 15 years experience in business planning. Currently, as Business Development and planning Manager for Best Foods, a $13 billion frozen foods manufacturer, I manage a department of five talented analysts responsible for all business development and planning activities for the corporation.

Our overall charter is to develop and recommend those business plans and strategies required to effectively manage the resources of the business and maximize return on the firm's capital investment. Some key results achieved include:

- Diversification into the frozen concentrate juice market through acquisition of two key companies (Results = 20% ROI in second year)

- Consolidation of Fresh Cut and Greens Divisions into single business (Results = $30 million annual overhead savings)

- Business expansion into Pacific Rim (Results = 60% annual growth rate with excellent profitability)

- Sale of Guerner Dairy Products Division (Results = immediate improvement of 10% to corporate profits)

I have long admired the Drumstix organization and would greatly appreciate the opportunity to be considered for this position. I feel that I am well prepared to take on this assignment and have the knowledge, skills and energy to make a significant contribution to your company.

I would welcome the chance to meet with you and the members of your senior management group for the purpose of further exploring the specifics of your requirements. I look forward to hearing from you shortly. Thank you.

Sincerely,

Marianne P. Butler

Marianne P. Butler

Enclosure

PATENT ATTORNEY

Corporate Legal Department of Internationally-known, Fortune 200 pharmaceutical company seeks experienced Patent Attorney for Washington-based corporate headquarters. Position reports to Senior Counsel-Patents.

We seek an attorney with an undergraduate degree in Chemistry, Chemical Engineering or Biology and at least 2 years patent experience in the pharmaceutical or chemical process industry.

We offer the opportunity for excellent professional growth, and provide highly competitive compensation and excellent benefits coverage.

Qualified professionals, please forward complete resume and cover letter stating current compensation level to:

Ms. Nadine S. Blackwell
Manager of Administrative Employment

Superior Pharmaceutical Corporation

10 Federation Avenue
Washington, DC 20036

Equal Opportunity Employer

PATRICK E. GEARHART
6233 Rose Tree Road
Columbia, MD 21106

March 29, 1998

Ms. Nadine S. Blackwell
Manager of Administrative Employment
Superior Pharmaceutical Corporation
10 Federation Avenue
Washington, DC 20036

Dear Ms. Blackwell:

When opening the current issue of *Legal Briefs*, I spotted your advertisement for the position of Patent Attorney. Although I have not been looking for a change, your ad did catch my attention. I would very much like to work in the pharmaceutical industry, and your firm is particularly attractive to me.

My credentials, as called for in your ad, include a B.S. in Chemistry from Cornell University and over two years in the chemical industry as a Patent Attorney. My law degree is from Georgetown University School of Law.

I am currently working in the Corporate Law Division of Ashland Chemical Company, where I am their principal attorney in the patent area. Ashland, as you may know, is a small $30 million manufacturer of intermediate chemicals sold primarily to the pharmaceutical industry. As such, I have had to learn a good deal about pharmaceutical manufacturing processes.

I feel my qualifications are an excellent match for your requirements, and I would appreciate the opportunity to meet with you and the members of your law staff to further discuss your requirements.

Thank you for your consideration. I look forward to hearing from you shortly.

Sincerely,

Patrick E. Gearhart

Patrick E. Gearhart

Enclosure

917 Cheswick Place
Rochester, NY 14602-1880

November 12, 1997

Box Y-222
The New York Times
New York, NY 10108

Dear Sir or Madam:

I was pleasantly surprised this morning to discover your advertisement for a Senior Vice President and General Counsel in *The New York Times* for two reasons. First, I have recently decided to make a career move. Second, I would appear to be well-suited to your requirements.

As Assistant General Counsel for Bristol Myers-Squibb, a $6 billion pharmaceutical and consumer products company, I report to the General Counsel and have managerial accountability for approximately half the Law Division (30 attorneys). For the last five years, my principal accountability has been to investigate and direct all major litigation work (several cases in the multi-million dollar range) covering a wide range of legal issues from antitrust cases, to consumer liability issues, to class action suits, to patent infringement suits, etc. I am proud to say that I have established a strong "winning" record over the years.

Interestingly, as called for in your ad, I have broad knowledge of corporate law to include both general business and patent law. My career includes five years in the patent area, three years as a legal specialist in human relations, and four years in real estate related areas. This experience, coupled with my litigation background, should make me a very desirable candidate for the position you are attempting to fill.

My resume is enclosed for your consideration. As requested, my compensation requirements include a base salary in the $175,000 to $200,000 range plus executive bonus.

Should you conclude that I am a viable candidate for this position, I would be pleased to meet with you and the senior members of your management team to further explore my qualifications at your convenience.

Thank you for your consideration, and I look forward to your reply.

Sincerely,

Jason P. Conroy

Jason P. Conroy

JPC/se

Enclosure

QUALITY MANAGER

We are a $200 million manufacturer of copper tubing sold to commercial developers and industrial OEM accounts.

We are in search of a Quality Manager for our copper refining and tube manufacturing facility located in Reading, Pennsylvania. this position reports to the Director of Operations and is responsible for managing the quality function for this 300 employee facility. Reporting to this position are 3 Quality Shift Supervisors and 2 Quality Laboratory Technicians.

The candidate we seek will have at least an Associate's degree in science (Engineering Technology, Physics or Chemistry) and a minimum of 5 years quality supervisory/ management experience in the metals refining/finishing industry. Must have experience working with engineering and operations personnel to establish the quality standards, inspection and laboratory testing procedures necessary to meet industry standards and customer specifications.

Qualified candidates are encouraged to submit resume and salary requirements to:

Personnel Director
DELUXE CONDUIT COMPANY
One Millwright Avenue
Syracuse, NY 10677

MARILYN D. ALFIERO

221 Ashton Road
Newark, NJ 07101
H: (201) 632-5706
O: (212) 449-6000

June 22, 1997

Personnel Director
Deluxe Conduit Company
One Millwright Avenue
Syracuse, NY 10677

Dear Sir or Madam:

This morning's *Newark Star Ledger* contained your advertisement for a Quality Manager, a position in which I would be very interested. Enclosed you will find a copy of my resume for review and consideration.

Your ad states that you seek at least an Associate's degree in science and a minimum of five years quality supervisory or management experience in the metals refining/finishing industry. My qualifications are:

- B.S., Metallurgy, University of Vermont, School of Mining

- Six years Quality experience, Revere Copper & Brass Co.
  - Two years - Manager of Quality Assurance
  - Four years - Quality Shift Supervisor

Further, as specified in your advertisement, the candidate must have experience working with engineering and operations personnel to establish the quality standards and inspection/laboratory test procedures to meet industry standards and customer specifications. My qualifications include:

- Extensive experience working with Engineering and Operations personnel in all areas related to Quality

- Publication of Quality Inspection and Testing Manual and training of all Quality and Operations personnel in proper inspection and testing methods

Hopefully, you will agree that I am well-qualified for your opening, and I will have the chance to further explore this position during a face-to-face interview at your facility. I would welcome such an opportunity to discuss your requirements in greater detail.

Thank you for your consideration, and I look forward to your reply.

Sincerely,

Marilyn D Alfiero

Marilyn D. Alfiero

Enclosure

DIRECTOR

TOTAL QUALITY MANAGEMENT

Leading manufacturer of quality men's shoes seeks Corporate Director of Total Quality Management. Position reports directly to the President.

This position will lead to the design and implementation of a corporate-wide total quality effort based upon the principles and beliefs of Dr. Edwards Deming.

Seek Ph.D. in Statistics with 10+ years experience in total quality field. Must have been key architect and facilitator of a major SPC-based quality initiative in a multi-plant manufacturing company.

In addition to technical skills, must exhibit strong interpersonal, communication and leadership skills. Must be able to effectively relate to wide range of people, from top management to hourly operators.

Highly competitive salary, performance bonus, and comprehensive benefits program are provided.

Send resume, including compensation requirements, to:

Mr. Saul Kirshman
Vice President Human Resources

FLORSCHEIM, INC.
1650 Laurel Avenue
Portland, ME 80116

LELAND S. BISHOP

806 Fern Ridge
Bridgeport, CT 06604

Home: (203)
(Office: (203)

June 16, 1998

Mr. Saul Kirshman
Vice President Human Resources
Florscheim, Inc.
1650 Laurel Avenue
Portland, ME 80116

Dear Mr. Kirshman:

The Classified Section of today's *Bridgeport Post* contained your advertisement for a Director of Total Quality. My qualifications appear to be an excellent match for this position, so I am enclosing my resume for your consideration.

I hold a Ph.D. in Statistics from the University of Illinois and, as called for in your ad, my qualifications include over ten years experience in the total quality field.

In my current position as Manager of Quality for Stafford, Inc. a $100 million manufacturer of men's clothing, I have successfully facilitated and led the department of a company-wide SPC-based quality initiative. This included implementation at three of our manufacturing sites.

In addition to my technical skills, I am considered to have strong interpersonal, communications and leadership skills. All of these characteristics were prerequisites to entering my current position, and have been critical qualifications needed for effective performance. The success of our current effort provides ample testimony to my strengths in these important areas.

I am a strong Deming advocate, and get excited about the opportunity to assume a Director level position in a company looking for key leadership in implementing a corporate-wide total quality effort based upon his teachings. I feel I have much to bring to Florscheim Shoes as a candidate, and could well have the overall knowledge and capability necessary to successfully lead your total quality effort.

I would encourage your strong consideration of my employment candidacy, and would hope that we would have the opportunity to meet shortly.

Thank you for your consideration, and I look forward to hearing from you.

Sincerely,

Leland S. Bishop

Leland S. Bishop

Enclosure

MANUFACTURING MANAGER

Poly-Foam, Inc. is a $20 million manufacturer of reticulated and unreticulated polyurethane foam sold to acoustical and filtration applications. We have experienced excellent growth and increased profitability over the last 5 years, and are planning a $5 million capital expansion this year.

We seek a talented, seasoned Manufacturing Manager for our two-plant, 110 employee operation. This position reports to the Executive Vice President and will manage a staff of 12 Manufacturing Shift Supervisors.

The successful candidate will hold a degree in Engineering (prefer Ch.E.) and at least 8 to 10 years management experience in the manufacture of polyurethane foam or other polymer-based products. Desire excellent interpersonal, communications and leadership skills. Prefer some prior plant start-up experience.

Excellent compensation and benefits package is provided.

For consideration, please forward complete resume and recent salary history to:

Manager of Human Resources
POLY-FOAM, INC.
400 Devon Park Drive
Greensboro, NC 27408

An Equal Opportunity Employer, M/F

ELIZABETH P. MASON
333 North Wilmont Street
Staunton, VA 24401
(703) 248-2693

August 21, 1998

Manager of Human Resources
Poly-Foam, Inc.
400 Devon Park Drive
Greensboro, NC 27408

Dear Sir or Madam:

The position of Manufacturing Manager, as advertised in the August 20th edition of *The Wall Street Journal*, is a surprisingly good match for my qualifications!

Consider the following:

- B.S. Chemical Engineering, George Washington University
- 15 years manufacturing experience - polyurethane foam
- Start-up experience as Plant Manager - Richmond Plant
- Excellent interpersonal, communications and leadership skills

In my current position as Manufacturing Manager for Johnson Foams, Inc., I manage an $18 million, three plant, 75 employee operation engaged in the manufacture of specialty polyurethane foams. During the last three years in this position, key accomplishments have included:

- Reduction in operating costs of 20%. (Annual Savings of $2 million)
- Increased Production throughout by 10%. (Annual Value of $1.2 million)
- Reduced staff by 5%. (Annual savings of $500,000)

Perhaps I could make similar contributions to your firm. I would appreciate the opportunity to meet with you and appropriate members of your executive team to further explore your requirements and my qualifications.

I look forward to your reply and hope that we will have the opportunity to meet in the near future. Thank you for your consideration.

Sincerely,

Elizabeth P. Mason

Elizabeth P. Mason

Enclosure

DIRECTOR OF MANUFACTURING

The Agricultural Products Division of our $3.8 billion, Indiana-based chemical company is looking for a talented Director of Manufacturing for its six-plant, 2,400 employee chemical manufacturing operation. This position reports to the Division President.

We seek a B.S.Ch.E. with 20+ years manufacturing experience in agricultural or specialty chemicals. Must demonstrate strong performance record in the profitable management of a sizeable, complex, multi-plant operation. Must also exhibit strong working knowledge of modern manufacturing concepts to include: JIT, MRP, SPC-based total quality and employee empowerment.

Conversion of culture from "top down" management approach to a socio-technical, systems-based operation will require appropriate management style conducive to successful leadership of this cultural shift.

Interested candidates should forward resume and compensation requirements to:

Mr. D. L. Crane
Vice President Operations

Quality Chemicals, Inc.
6911 Hillsdale Court
Indianapolis, IN 47101

An Equal Opportunity Employer, M/F

ANTHONY P. FITZGIBBONS

1733 East Gulf Road
Spokane, WA 99210

September 16, 1998

Mr. D. L. Crane
Vice President Operations
Quality Chemicals, Inc.
6911 Hillsdale Court
Indianapolis, IN 47101

Dear Mr. Crane:

If, as your September 16th ad in the *Spokesman-Review* suggests, you are looking for a top-flight executive to lead your manufacturing function, you may want to give my credentials careful consideration. I appear to be an excellent match for your current requirements.

Please consider the following relevant highlights of my qualifications:

- B.S. Chemical Engineering, Stanford University

- Total of 26 years Chemical Manufacturing experience (8 years agricultural chemicals)

- Management of a $2.6 billion, four plant, 1,600 employee, specialty chemicals operation

- First-hand experience with modern manufacturing concepts/approaches including: JIT, MRP, SPC-based Total Quality, etc.

- Extensive training in, and experience with, Socio-technical Systems Approach to Management (implemented across all operations)

- Strong history of successful financial performance

The enclosed resume will provide you with the specifics of my manufacturing management experience and accomplishments.

Should you agree that I am a strong candidate for your requirements, I would welcome the opportunity to meet with you personally to explore the possible contributions that I can make to Quality Chemicals.

My compensation requirements are a base salary in the $125K to $135K range plus bonus.

Thank you for your consideration.

Sincerely,

Anthony P. Fitzgibbons

Anthony P. Fitzgibbons

Enclosure

GENERAL MANAGER

We are part of a division of a world-wide supplier of technology, products and services for the energy market. Currently, we have unprecedented opportunity for growth and are searching for a General Manager to direct the operation of our two manufacturing facilities in Southern Texas.

This highly visible position will be filled by a candidate who has a proven track record in managing manufacturing operations at the $100 to $150 million level and who will have repeatedly demonstrated the ability to cost effectively increase velocity and throughput in operations. Position requires a degree in engineering or business, a solid record of accomplishment in increasingly responsible positions in a manufacturing environment, and excellent communications skills.

Qualified candidates are encouraged to send their resume and salary history in confidence to:

Box 188Y
HOUSTON CHRONICLE
801 Texas Avenue
Houston, TX 77002

SCOTT M. BEATTY

162 Monument Lane, Beaumont, TX 75227

April 13, 1998

Box 188Y
Houston Chronicle
801 Texas Avenue
Houston, TX 77002

Dear Sir or Madam:

Today's *Houston Chronicle* contains your advertisement for a General Manager, along with a brief description of the requirements for this position. My background appears to satisfy your requirements rather well, so I am enclosing my resume for your review and consideration.

I am currently Group Manufacturing Manager for a $155 million, three plant division of Charman Manufacturing, a leader in the field of precision specialty gauges for the nuclear power industry. I hold a dual degree in Mechanical and Electrical Engineering at the bachelor's level. Evidence of my ability to be a solid contributor to business results includes:

- Increased production output by 28% through redesign of manufacturing equipment layout (annual value of $5.6 million)

- Decreased manufacturing costs by 21% over three years through reduction in manpower, improved inventory planning and manufacturing scheduling, and reduction in spare parts inventory ($6.3 million annual savings)

- Implemented total quality program resulting in 96% reduction in scrap and a 98% reduction in customer complaints ($1.4 million annual savings)

These are but a few of the key results I have achieved on behalf of my employers throughout my career in manufacturing. Additional achievements are detailed in the enclosed resume.

As my resume will confirm, I have experienced excellent career progression and have advanced rather rapidly to positions of increasing responsibility in the manufacturing field. Additionally, I am credited with having strong communications and leadership skills.

My current annual compensation is $115,000. This includes a base salary of $95,000 plus a bonus of $20,000.

I would welcome the opportunity to meet with you for the purpose of exploring the contributions I could make to your company.

Thank you for your consideration, and I look forward to your reply.

Sincerely,

Scott M. Beatty

Scott M. Beatty

Enclosure

DUANE O. ANDREWS, III

177 Oasis Avenue
Mesa, AZ 60221

Home: (602) 579-3762
Office (602) 403-2110

July 16, 1997

Box P-100
The Arizona Republic
120 E. Van Buren
Phoenix, AZ 85004

Dear Sir of Madam:

Your July 16th advertisement in *The Arizona Republic* for a President & CEO reads like a carbon copy of my credentials. Perhaps we should meet to discuss the possibilities for a successful relationship.

Please consider the following qualifications as they relate to your needs:

- M.S. Environmental Engineering, B.S. Chemical Engineering

- MBA, Finance, Columbia University

- 20 years total experience - technical consulting
  10 years experience - environmental consulting
  8 years senior management - $120 million firm

- Managed rapid-growth business units expanding at annual growth rate of 45% +

- Heavily involved in leading business growth through both acquisition and new business development

In my current position as Executive Vice President of Enviro-Tech, a $130 million environmental engineering consulting firm, I am responsible to the President for the daily operating results of the firm's consulting divisions. I am also a member of the Senior Executive Committee, and am considered to be a key force in formulation of both long and short-range business strategy.

May I suggest that we meet to further discuss your requirements? I believe that I am uniquely suited to your needs and have the knowledge and leadership skills necessary to successfully lead your business.

I look forward to hearing from you shortly. Thank you.

Sincerely,

Duane O. Andrews, III

Enclosure

5

Networking Cover Letters

No good book on cover letters could possibly be complete without a chapter on the subject of the networking cover letter.

Several studies have measured the effectiveness of various job-hunting sources. All agree on one thing—employment networking, by far, is the single most productive source for finding jobs! In fact, various studies have shown that between 63 and 75 percent of all jobs are actually found through use of the networking process.

WHAT IS EMPLOYMENT NETWORKING?

Employment networking is the process by which a job seeker makes use of personal contacts to find employment. The idea is to use personal contacts to arrange introductions to others who could be influential in helping with a job search.

The networking process, in principle, works much like the popular chain-letter concept (or cell-division theory). It allows you to exponentially expand your own personal contacts by tapping into the social networks of others. The process looks something like this:

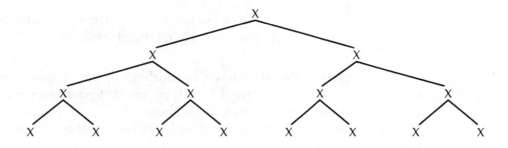

If each contact you make in the chain leads to only two other contacts, the two initial contacts can quickly multiply to eight contacts, as indicated by the diagram. By asking each contact to introduce you to two or three other persons who might help you with advice or assistance, it is possible to eventually have several hundred others actively involved in some way with your job search. This extremely powerful job-hunting technique has demonstrated its effectiveness time and time again!

It is not our purpose here to train you in the use of the networking process. If you need help in this area, refer to one of my other books, *Get the Right Job in 60 Days or Less* (Wiley), which provides over 180 pages on the effective use of the networking process. The purpose of this chapter is to assist you with the composition of effective networking cover letters that can help to facilitate the employment networking approach.

PURPOSE OF NETWORKING COVER LETTER

Essentially, the purpose of the networking cover letter is threefold:

1. Set the stage for a personal introduction.
2. Transmit your resume.
3. Acquaint the person with your qualifications in advance of your networking contact (that is, phone call or meeting).

The networking cover letter is an important document in helping the networking process to flow properly. A well-designed, well-written cover letter will go a long way toward setting the stage for your networking contact. If well done, the letter will accomplish the following:

1. Make the person whom you are contacting feel comfortable—willing to open up and share valuable information (that is, job leads and names of key contacts) with you.
2. Provide sufficient information about your qualifications and job-search objectives to allow the contact to make intelligent recommendations to you.
3. Provide sufficient information to allow the contact to intelligently discuss your qualifications and job interests with others.

Conversely, if the cover letter is poorly designed or poorly written, most (if not all) of these potential benefits will be lost and your targeted contact will not be in a position to provide meaningful help.

A well-written networking cover letter is critical to the success of your job-hunting campaign.

ELEMENTS OF NETWORKING COVER LETTER

The following is a summary of the basic elements of a well-written networking cover letter:

1. Personalized opening paragraph to include:
   a. Name of the person who has referred you;
   b. Nature of your relationship with this person;
   c. Some personal comments (where appropriate).
2. Explanation of how referral came about (optional).
3. Reason for job/career change (optional).
4. Reference to known job opening (if one exists).
5. Indirect networking approach (if no known job exists).
6. Brief summary of qualifications (and reference to enclosed resume).
7. Action statement—designed to initiate next action (that is, phone call or personal meeting), with contact information.
8. Statement of appreciation (thank you).

The cover letter samples that comprise the rest of this chapter should provide you with an ample array of models from which to choose in tailoring your own networking cover letters.

ROBERT P. GOLDHORN
2606 Highland Avenue
Baton Rouge, LA 70809
(505) 924-6607

October 15, 1998

Mr. Patrick C. Gallagher
National Sales Manager
Whalen Corporation
2015 Bourbon Street
New Orleans, LA 66393

Dear Patrick:

Jerry Currie mentioned your name to me the other day and strongly suggested I contact you. Jerry and I grew up together in Little Rock, Arkansas, and still see one another frequently.

From what Jerry tells me, you are very active as an officer in the American Society of Heating, Refrigeration and Air Conditioning and know a number of sales executives in the industry. As a result, he felt you might be willing to lend me a hand.

Carrier Corporation, my current employer, has recently been sold to United Technologies. United has its own sales organization, and will simply fold Carrier's product line into their existing line. Unfortunately, this means that my job, along with the jobs of 25 other Sales Representatives, has been eliminated.

As the enclosed resume shows, I have a B.A. degree in Marketing from Ohio State, and have been working as a Sales Representative in the HVAC industry for two years.

Although I certainly would not expect you to be aware of a specific job opportunity for me, I would appreciate it if you could spend an hour or so with me over lunch. I would value any general thoughts and advice you might have concerning my job hunting campaign. Jerry seemed to feel you might be very helpful in this regard.

I will plan to call you next Monday to see when it might be convenient for us to meet. I would very much appreciate your counsel. Thank you.

Sincerely,

Bob Goldhorn

Robert P. Goldhorn

Enclosure

621 Edgewater Drive
Glenview, IL 60025

August 15 1998

Ms. Theresa McDevitt
Executive Director
American Marketing Association
335 Park Avenue
New York, NY 16284

Dear Ms. McDevitt:

As the chief executive officer of the nation's largest
professional marketing association, I felt you might be in a
position to provide some excellent counsel and advice. I have
been an Association member since 1989, and have been active on
various regional committees. You may recall, we met briefly
over lunch at last year's national meeting in Dallas.

I am currently Vice President of Sales for Zenith Corporation,
a $1.5 billion manufacturer of consumer electronics and
furniture sold to OEM accounts. In this capacity, I manage an
international salesforce of over 150 employees and market our
products in some 16 countries. A confidential copy of my
resume is enclosed for your reference.

Although I have had quite a successful career to-date, some
recent top management changes at Zenith have caused me to
rethink my objectives. As a result, I have decided to make a
change and am currently conducting a highly confidential job
search. Zenith is unaware of my decision.

I would appreciate if you could spend a few minutes with me on
the phone sometime in the next few days. I would value your
observations and insight concerning current national trends in
the sales profession and how these might impact my job search.
Additionally, I would welcome any general thoughts and ideas
that you might have regarding my search.

I will plan to call you shortly, and look forward to our
conversation. In the meantime, I would appreciate any thought
that you might give to this matter.

Thank you.

Very truly yours,

Patricia A. Helms

Patricia A. Helms

Enclosure

JAMES R. REARDON

212 Maplewood Road   Home: (617) 575-8859
Cambridge, MA 01742   Office: (617) 630-1130

March 22, 1999

Mr. Bruce J. Reinhardt
Brand Manager
CertainTeed Corporation
570 East Swedesford Road
Wayne, PA 19087

Dear Bruce:

I am writing to you at the suggestion of Roger Dolby, who I understand is a former neighbor of yours. Roger and I were fraternity brothers at Georgia Tech, and have stayed in touch over the years.

The other night, over dinner, Roger and I were discussing my plans for a career change and your name came up as someone who has a strong professional network in the consumer marketing field. Roger felt, as a result, you might be in a position to assist me.

Bruce, don't get me wrong. I am not expecting that you would have a job for me, nor would I expect that you would be aware of one. Instead, what I am hoping is that you might be willing to share the names of a few good contacts in the consumer marketing field -- persons, like you, who are professionally active and know others in the field. I would also appreciate any general suggestions you might have concerning my job hunting campaign.

I have taken the liberty of enclosing my resume for your reference. In short, I have a B.A. in Business from Georgia Tech and three years experience as a Market Analyst with Armstrong World Industries. I am seeking a similar position with a major consumer products company, preferable on the East Coast.

I will plan to give you a call sometime during the next week, and would hope that you will be able to spend a few minutes with me. I would greatly appreciate your advice and counsel.

Thank you.

Sincerely,

James R. Reardon

JRR/ae

Enclosure

ELAINE C. MARKESON

722 Peachtree Lane
Atlanta, GA 40434

Home: (404) 454-7665
Office: (404) 231-1900

February 22, 1998

Mr. James M. Borman
President
JMB Controls, Inc.
4335 Main Street
Atlanta, GA 43602

Dear Mr. Borman:

Mike Cullen, a tennis partner and friend, thought it would be a good idea for me to contact you. Mike and I play doubles together at Green Valley Country Club where we also serve on the Board of Directors. I understand, from Mike, that you're quite a tennis player yourself. He tells me that the last time the two of you met on the courts you thoroughly humiliated him with your power serve.

During tennis last week, I mentioned to Mike that I would be leaving my position as Director of Marketing for General Precision. General Precision, as you know, is a leading manufacturer of specialty control instrumentation for the chemical process industry.

As President of a major player in the process control field, Mike seemed to feel you would be an excellent person to talk with about my career change. He tells me that you are a very knowledgeable colleague and might have some good advice that would be helpful to my job search. I would very much value your counsel in this regard.

I have enclosed a copy of my resume to facilitate our discussion, and would appreciate if you might have a moment to look it over.

Knowing that you likely have a busy schedule, I will contact your secretary early next week to see if we can establish a convenient time for us to talk. I look forward to our conversation, and would very much appreciate your advice and counsel.

Thank you.

Sincerely,

Elaine C. Markeson

Elaine C. Markeson

ECM/mf

Enclosure

DAVID M. CARMICHAEL

176 Rutherford Way
Boise, ID 83702

Home: (208) 535-2708
Office: (208) 891-1470

July 28, 1999

Mr. John D. Sebera
Director of Manufacturing
Stokley-Van Camp, Inc.
321 North Clark Street
Chicago, IL 60610

Dear Mr. Sebera:

When searching through the *Sigma Chi Alumni Directory*, I came across your name. (I am a 1995 graduate of the University of Illinois, where I was Vice President of the local Sigma Chi Chapter). I am writing in hopes that you might be in a position to provide me with some advice and assistance.

I have recently elected to make a career change, and am looking to find a new position in manufacturing in the food and/or beverage industry. Since graduating with a B.S. in Industrial Engineering in 1995, I have been in manufacturing with Ore-Ida Foods. Most recently, I have been Operations Manager for a 150 employee packaging operation here in Boise.

Although Ore-Ida has been good to me, and I have learned much in the four years since graduation, I do miss the Illinois area. Both my wife and I are from the Greater Chicago area and would love to return, provided I am able to find a comparable position to the one I now hold at Ore-Ida.

Mr. Sebera, as a member of Sigma Chi and as a manufacturing executive with a major food company in the Illinois area, I thought you might be a good person to contact. Although it is unlikely that Stokley-Van Camp would coincidentally be looking for someone with my background, I thought perhaps you might be in a position to introduce me to other manufacturing executives in the Chicago area through whom I might network in finding a suitable opening. In addition, I would greatly appreciate any suggestions you might personally have concerning my job search.

I have taken the liberty of enclosing my resume for your reference. I would very much appreciate if you could spare a few minutes with me on the phone to discuss this matter.

I will plan to call your secretary to see if I can coordinate a time that would be convenient to your schedule.

Thank you for your assistance, and I look forward to talking with you.

Sincerely,

David M. Carmichael

David M. Carmichael

Enclosure

CHERYL A. HUNDLEY
570 Waterloo Road
Rockford, IL 61103
(518) 767-9013

February 23, 1998

Mr. Stephen J. Tomasko
Vice President of Manufacturing
Bowmar Instrument Corporation
4080 North 50th Street, Suite 525
Phoenix, Arizona 85015

Dear Steve:

I am writing to you as a fellow member of the American Manufacturers' Association to request your assistance and advice concerning a career change that I am planning. You may recall, we were introduced by Ann Johnson at the last AMA meeting in Boston, and talked at length about implementation of TQC at the operating level. I enjoyed our conversation very much.

Currently, I am Vice President of Operations for Atwood Industries, a $350 million manufacturer of industrial valves. Although a fine company, unfortunately Atwood is family-owned and literally all senior management personnel are members of the Lawler family. This does not bode well for long-term career growth, so I have quietly opted to pursue a career search to find an environment that offers brighter long-term growth prospects.

Steve, although I am not expecting that you will be aware of a specific opening for me, I would very much appreciate the opportunity to talk with you more broadly about my job search campaign. I would certainly value your observations about the general market as well as any ideas you might have that would be helpful to my job hunting approach.

I am enclosing my resume for your review, and will plan to give you a call shortly.

By the way, Ann was aware that I would be contacting you and said to say "hello". She mentioned that she was planning to look you up at the AMA meeting next month in San Diego, and has some interesting information for you concerning the problem you were having with SPC training of operating personnel.

Steve, I greatly appreciate your help concerning my job search and look forward to our discussion. Thank you.

Very truly yours,

Cheryl A. Hundley

Cheryl A. Hundley

CAH:ag

Enclosure

JOSEPH J. HONEYCUTT

901 Eddystone Avenue, Bloomington, MN 55420

August 15, 1998

Ms. Janet Segawa
Engineering Manager
Honeywell, Inc.
95 Edgewood Avenue
New Britain, CT 06051

Dear Ms. Segawa:

Sheri Foster, one of my associates here at The Toro Company, suggested that I contact you. Sheri and I have jointly worked on various engineering projects here at Toro's small motors plant, and have gotten to know each other quite well. She tells me that she had worked two summers for you as a co-op student while attending Hartford University.

Ms. Segawa, after considerable soul-searching, I have decided to make a career change. I have spent the last two years since earning my engineering degree from the University of Minnesota working as a Design Engineer on small motors. Quite frankly, I have not found this work particularly interesting, and would much prefer working in the energy-related field on larger equipment such as industrial boilers, heat exchangers, etc.

Sheri tells me you direct an engineering department responsible for design of large boilers and pressure vessels. It is for this reason that she suggested I contact you.

Although you may not have an opening at Honeywell for someone with my credentials, both Sheri and I felt you might have some ideas and suggestions on how to make the transition to the energy-related equipment field. I know, with two years experience in the design of small motors, this may not be an easy transition for me to make. I would therefore very much value your advice and counsel on this subject.

I have enclosed an informational copy of my resume for your review, and would like to give you a call sometime during the next week or so. Perhaps I could prearrange an appropriate time to call through your secretary.

I appreciate your help in this matter and hope that your busy schedule will allow us to talk in the near future.

Sincerely,

Joseph J. Honeycutt

Joseph J. Honeycutt

Enclosure

LINDA S. COLLIER
4153 Sunset Ridge
Cambridge, MA 06017

January 15, 1999

Dr. Neil Loftiss
Senior Vice President - Technology
ACS Industries, Inc.
P.O. Box 7000
Atlanta, GA 40344

Dear Neil:

Bob Price, a close friend of mine, suggested I contact you. Bob and I have adjoining slips at
Boston's Old Harbor Marina, where our families have spent several summer weekends sailing
together -- I understand that you enjoy a bit of sailing as well.

Last weekend, while at Moon Island, I mentioned to Bob that I have decided to make a career
move. Since my background is in senior engineering management, Bob suggested that I might
want to contact you to see if you have any thoughts on this matter.

I have an M.S. in Chemical Engineering from Worcester Polytechnic Institute and over 20
years engineering experience in the chemical process industry. Currently, I am Director of
Engineering for Cambrex Corporation's Polymers Division, where I direct a 250 employee
central engineering group concerned with the engineering design, installation and start-up of
major polymer manufacturing facilities. A copy of my resume is enclosed, providing you with
further details of my background.

As it turns out, Neil, I will be in Atlanta for two weeks starting February 1. Perhaps, if your
schedule would permit, we could meet over dinner. I would welcome the opportunity to
discuss my job search with you and would appreciate your general counsel and advice on this
matter. I will call your office early next week to see if your schedule will allow us to get
together.

Thank you for your help with this matter, Neil, and I look forward to the possibility of meeting
with you personally.

Very truly yours,

Linda S. Collier

Linda S. Collier

LSC:dae

Enclosure

722 Wakefield Avenue
Cheswick, RI 02895

September 15, 1999

Dr. Elizabeth A. Gilbert
Director of Absorbant Technology
The Procter & Gamble Company
One P&G Plaza, Box 599
Cincinnati, OH 45201

Dear Dr. Gilbert:

Ross Glatzer, a former member of your technical staff, has suggested I contact you. Ross and I are colleagues and have worked together in the Product Development Group of Bonded Fibers, Inc. for the last two years.

Dr. Gilbert, Ross has told me about some of the work that your group has been doing on the development of new, super absorbant systems for use in the development of incontinence diapers. He thought my recent work involving the use of polymer-based gels for super absorbant applications may be of interest to your organization.

I have recently made a decision to leave Bonded Fibers, to seek employment in the Technology Department of a larger corporation, where there is greater emphasis on basic research. It would appear that my background could be an excellent fit with some of the areas on which you are working. I am therefore enclosing a copy of my resume for your review and consideration.

Perhaps, if you do not currently have an opening on your staff, you would be kind enough to share some of your general thoughts and ideas on others with whom I should be in contact in the field of absorbancy. I would sincerely welcome your advice and counsel in this regard.

I will plan to call your office next Monday, to arrange a convenient time for us to talk. I would greatly appreciate any assistance that you could provide regarding this matter.

Thank you very much.

Sincerely,

Patricia J. Kilpatrick

Patricia J. Kilpatrick

Enclosure

JOHN C. MORRISON, Ph.D.

1062 Greenhill Lane
Paramus, NJ 08090

Home: (908) 391-2359
Office: (908) 575-6722

June 23, 1998

Mr. Lawrence K. Trowbridge, Jr.
President
FMC Corporation
16th and Arch Streets
Philadelphia, PA 19119

Dear Larry:

I am writing to you at the suggestion of Mark Boden, a close friend and former classmate of mine at Cambridge University. Mark and I were having lunch together last Wednesday, when I mentioned to him that I was planning to make a career change. He suggested that perhaps you might be an excellent person to contact concerning my plans because of your many contacts in the chemical industry and related areas.

Larry, I doubt that you would be aware of a specific job opportunity for me, however, I would certainly appreciate the chance to talk with you about my job search in a more general sense. Mark tells me that you have been very active in various industry associations and, in your current capacity, stay very much on top of what is happening in the industry. Perhaps you would be kind enough to share some of your observations about current industry trends and events which might impact my job search. In any event, I would be most appreciative of any general thoughts and ideas you might have on this subject.

Enclosed please find a copy of my resume for your review. Briefly, I have a Ph.D. in Polymer Engineering from Cornell University and over 25 years research experience in the development of pigments and dyes sold to industrial applications. Most recently, I have been Vice President of Technology for Ashland Chemical Company, responsible for a 50 employee research department in the development of specialty dyes and pigments sold to the paint industry. I am sure you are familiar with our firm.

Larry, I would very much appreciate the opportunity to discuss this matter with you, and would sincerely welcome your insights concerning both the industry and my job search.

I will plan to give your office a call next week, and look forward to the opportunity to talk with you personally. Mark has told me a great deal about you.

Thank you for your willingness to be of assistance, and I look forward to our conversation.

Sincerely,

John Morrison

John C. Morrison

Enclosure

DIANE T. RUSSELL

936 Rutledge Avenue
Lincoln, NE 68508

Home: (402) 727-4072
Office: (402) 466-9380

October 14, 1998

Ms. Corinne D. Chapin
Manager of Accounting
Guilford Manufacturing, Inc.
4300 Commerce Square
Pittsburgh, PA 15230

Dear Corinne:

I was taking with Anita Wallgren the other evening, and she suggested that I give you a call. Anita and I have been very active in the local Chapter of the National Business Women's Association, and have done a lot of scheming together on ways that women might be more assertive in taking control of their careers, and not simply taking what is handed to them.

I guess I have taken a lot of our conversations to heart, and have now decided that it is time to take charge of my own career. Unfortunately, I find myself in a very male-dominated environment here at Delaney Roe & Company, and will need to make a career move if I am going to expect to move ahead with both my career and professional development.

Delaney Roe is a small but high-quality CPA firm located here in Lincoln. They have an excellent reputation and a strong base of medium-sized manufacturing and service clients. I joined them as an Auditor in their Auditing Department two years ago, following receipt of my Accounting degree from the University of Omaha. A copy of my resume is enclosed for your reference.

Corinne, I would like to make the transition from public accounting to a position in manufacturing cost accounting with a medium to large manufacturing company, where there would be reasonable expectation for career growth based upon contribution and performance. My current compensation is $35,000 annually.

As an accounting manager for a medium-sized manufacturing firm, Anita seemed to feel you would be an excellent person for me to talk with on this matter. I understand that you, yourself, successfully made a similar transition a couple of years ago. As a result, you might be in a position to share some of your observations and insights.

I would really appreciate an opportunity to talk with you, and would sincerely welcome any overall suggestions that you might have regarding my career search. Perhaps I could call your secretary to arrange for a time that would be convenient to your schedule.

Thank you for your help, Corinne. Anita has told me so much about you, and I really look forward to our conversation.

Sincerely,

Diane T. Russell

Diane T. Russell

Enclosure

EVELYN M. WHITING

415 Woodhaven Drive
Morristown, NJ 08998

Home: (908) 377-5971
Office: (908) 692-2205

May 16, 1999

Mr. Samuel T. Parker
Senior Partner
Arthur Andersen & Company
200 West 57th Street
New York, NY 10026

Dear Sam:

I can see by your new title that things are going rather well for you at Arthur Andersen. Congratulations!

It seems like only yesterday that you and I were talking about your desire to make a move from manufacturing to the world of the "Big 6." I guess the introduction that I arranged for you with Allen Fry was just what you needed to get your career really rolling. I'm glad that things have worked out so well. It's always refreshing to see talented people rise to the top!

Sam, I only wish that my own career was doing as well. Although I really can't complain about having finally "arrived," so to speak, as C.F.O. of Manville Corporation, a recent change in the top management of the business has me concerned. As you know, Allen Dunlap has just been named President here at Manville. Although he is certainly a nice guy, I really don't believe he has the candle power to pull Manville out of the slide it has been experiencing in recent years. As a result, I feel it is time to start actively thinking about a serious career move.

I was wondering what your schedule might look like for lunch sometime in the next week or so. I would really like to get together with you to see what ideas you may have concerning my job search. My decision is highly confidential, of course, and I'm going to need to be most discreet in how I go about doing this. I would welcome your advice and counsel in this regard.

Why don't I give Eileen a call to see what we can set up? I would really appreciate your help on this, and look forward to our conversation.

Thanks, Sam, and I look forward to seeing you.

Sincerely,

Evelyn M. Whiting

Evelyn M. Whiting

P.S. I've enclosed a reference copy of my "draft" resume.

DENNIS E. HUEBENER

74335 East Panama Street
Sacramento, CA 91636

August 29, 1998

Mr. Lawrence D. Robinson
Manager of Financial Planning
Potter & Brumfield, Inc.
324 Ryan Avenue
St. Paul, MN 55164

Dear Larry:

It has been about two years since our last contact, but I'm sure you will remember the work that we did together on the proposed Sinclair merger. At the time, as you will likely recall, I was working as the Senior Analyst for R.L. Polk & Company on the project.

Larry, unfortunately, the current recession has not been kind to Polk & Company. There hasn't exactly been a plethora of merger and acquisition activity lately, and Polk has just announced its decision to cease operations effective October 15th. Thus, I am in search of a new career opportunity.

As you may remember, Larry, I hold an MBA from the Wharton School, where my major was Finance. I have been working as a financial analyst for Polk since June of 1995 (following graduation), principally focusing on providing technical support to client management in the financial evaluation of proposed M&A's. I have enclosed an informational copy of my resume to provide you with further details.

I am planning to be in the St. Paul area next week on business and was wondering if we might be able to meet. I would really appreciate some general advice and counsel concerning my job search, and thought perhaps we might do this over dinner, provided your schedule will permit. If not, maybe we can compare schedules and find a time that better fits your requirements.

Larry, I really enjoyed working with you on the Sinclair project, and came to have a great deal of respect for your knowledge of corporate finance. I would very much value your advice and counsel concerning my career, and hope that your schedule will allow us to meet. I will call you later this week to see when we might get together.

Thanks, Larry, for your help in this matter, and I look forward to seeing you again.

Sincerely,

Dennis

Dennis E. Huebener

DEH/aw

Enclosure

TIMOTHY P. NOLAN

5226 Diamond Drive, Indianapolis, Indiana 44304

July 31, 1999

Mr. Dale H. Gibbons
Chief Financial Officer
Sharp Electronics
One Presidential Industrial Park
Benton Harbor, MI 49022

Dear Mr. Gibbons:

Your name was given to me by Bob Beavins, President of the Indianapolis Rotary Club. I understand that the two of you were neighbors and used to do a lot of sailing together when Bob lived in Benton Harbor. Bob and I have worked together on several Rotary projects over the last three years, and have gotten to know one another quite well.

During last Wednesday's Rotary meeting, I mentioned to Bob that I was planning to make a career change. Since I have a strong background in finance, he seemed to feel that I should contact you, and suggested that I use his name in doing so.

As summarized on the enclosed resume, I hold an MBA in Finance from the University of Chicago. After nearly 20 years in the Corporate Finance Department of Raytheon, Inc. I moved to Indianapolis as Director of Corporate Finance for Compu-Tech Corporation, a $600 million manufacturer of computer components. This has not proven to be the opportunity initially presented to me by Compu-Tech, and I have thus decided to return to the corporate financial world of the major corporation.

Although it is unlikely that you will be aware of a specific job opportunity for me, I would appreciate the opportunity to meet with you briefly to discuss my career plans and to benefit from any general advice and counsel that you might provide in this regard. It would also be valuable to get your insight concerning the state of the electronics/communications industry and the prospects for developing a fruitful career as a senior financial executive in this industry segment.

Realizing that you have a very busy schedule, I am fully prepared to adjust my own schedule accordingly. Perhaps, if convenient, we might even meet over an early breakfast. In any event, I will plan to call your secretary early next week to see if a convenient time might be worked out.

Mr. Gibbons, I really appreciate your help with my career search and look forward to the prospect of meeting with you personally. Thank you for your help in this matter.

Sincerely,

Timothy P. Nolan

Timothy P. Nolan

TPN/smc

Enclosure

ALICE M. COLEMAN
6244 Evergreen Court
Canton, Ohio 44720
(216) 494-8033

September 28, 1999

Mr. J. Brian Schaeffer
Manager of Human Resources
Hoover Company
2000 N. 59th Street
Philadelphia, PA 19132

Dear Mr. Schaeffer:

You may recall that I was a Human Resources Intern at Hoover's Corporate Benefits Department two years ago, while a senior at Drexel University. I certainly appreciated the opportunity to have lunch with you during my internship and valued your overall suggestions concerning my career in the field of Human Resources.

Since I had particularly enjoyed my internship, I was disappointed to learn that there were no entry-level opportunities available in Human Resources at the time of graduation from Drexel last year. Consequently, I took a position as Human Resources Administrator with Warren Manufacturing Company here in Canton. My enclosed resume provides further details regarding this position.

Mr. Schaeffer, I would very much like to return to the Philadelphia area since my family, and many of my closest friends reside in the Greater Philadelphia area. I am writing, therefore, to inquire if there are any entry-level openings on your staff for which I might be considered. Down deep, I still have a strong interest in working for Hoover Company.

In the event that there are no appropriate openings available at this time, I was wondering if you or any of your staff members could be of assistance to me in my effort to return to Philadelphia. Perhaps you are aware of others who are looking for someone with my credentials, or persons with whom I should be talking, who could be of assistance in my job search. Any general suggestions you might have in this regard would be greatly appreciated.

I will plan to call you sometime in the next few days and would hope that you might have a few moments to spend with me by phone. I really enjoyed our brief relationship and would value any advice and/or counsel you might be able to provide on this topic.

Thank you very much for your help and I look forward to speaking with you shortly.

Sincerely,

Alice M. Coleman

Alice M. Coleman

Enclosure

617 Hemlock Lane
Bakersfield, CA 90232

October 30, 1998

Mr. John W. Sullivan
Senior Vice President
Human Resources Department
Rush Industries, Inc.
One Mason Drive
P.O. Box 4000
Los Angeles, CA 90336

Dear Mr. Sullivan:

As Chapter President of the Human Resources Management Association for the Greater Los Angeles Metro Area, you are likely to be aware of senior-level human resources openings from time to time. I am therefore contacting you to see if you might have some suggestions concerning my job search.

I am currently Vice President of Human Resources for Butler Manufacturing, a $1.2 billion, 7,000 employee manufacturer of radar components. In my position, I report to the President of Butler and have world-wide responsibility for direction of the Company's Human Resources function. Details of my qualifications are shown on the enclosed resume.

My decision to leave Butler is highly confidential, and I am therefore being particularly discreet with regard to my job search efforts.

I am seeking a senior-level Human Resources position with a large manufacturing company, where I will be a member of the senior management team and have broad strategic responsibilities for contributing to the overall direction of the business. My compensation requirements are in the $150,000+ range.

I will plan to touch base with you shortly to determine if you are aware of any openings at this level that would be worth my pursuing. Should you not be aware of any appropriate openings, I would sincerely appreciate any thoughts you might have concerning either my resume or my job hunting strategy. Additionally, perhaps you may be aware of other individuals, with whom I should be in contact, who may be aware of appropriate openings at this level. In any event, I would welcome any ideas and/or assistance you might be able to provide to me.

Thank you very much for your willingness to help, and I look forward to speaking with you personally.

Sincerely,

Nicholas D. Paine

Nicholas D. Paine

NDP/sea

Enclosure

MALCOME J. SNOWDEN

145 East 42nd Street
Boston, MA 02120
(617)353-9217

June 22, 1998

Collette M. Taylor
Director of Corporate Planning
DEP Chemical Corporation
One Liberty Square
Boston, MA 02107

Dear Ms. Taylor:

I have just completed an MBA in Financial Planning at Boston College. Your name was given to me by Jerry Lucas, Vice President of Operations, who suggested I contact you. Mr. Lucas and my father, Donald Snowden, are close personal friends and graduated from Oxford University together.

As my resume will show, I am an honors graduate and hold an undergraduate degree in Mechanical Engineering. My credentials include nearly a year's worth of experience as a Financial Analyst in the Corporate Planning Department of Eaton Corporation, a $700 million British-owned chemical manufacturing company. During this time, I was instrumental in assisting Eaton in the evaluation of several potential acquisition candidates here in the U.S. I left Eaton to complete my final year of graduate study at Boston College.

Mr. Lucas indicated that he thought you might be looking for someone with my credentials for your Corporate Planning Department. If not, however, he felt that you might be willing to provide me with some suggestions and ideas concerning my job search. In particular, he seemed to feel that you might have some ideas about key persons with whom I should be in contact in the chemical industry.

Since I live here in Boston, it would be quite easy for me to come to your office for a meeting at a time that is convenient to you. I would certainly welcome the opportunity for such a meeting and would greatly appreciate your general advice and counsel concerning my job search. Hopefully, you will have some time in your busy schedule to meet with me.

Recognizing that you may be difficult to reach, I will plan to contact your secretary in an effort to arrange a convenient time for us to get together. I am totally flexible and would be pleased to meet either during or outside of normal business hours.

Thank you for your assistance, and I look forward to the possibility of meeting with you personally.

Sincerely,

Malcome J Snowden

Malcome J. Snowden

Enclosure

GLORIA A. WALDBRIDGE

11301 Springfield Road
Laurel, Maryland 20708

Home: (301) 688-9259
Office: (301) 779-4018

January 2, 1999

Dr. Craig J. Aiken
Professor & Chairman
Department of Economics
University of Pennsylvania
Wharton School of Business
3400 Spruce Street, 4th Floor
Philadelphia, PA 19104

Dear Dr. Aiken:

I was speaking to Eric Hollingsworth of Fleer Corporation the other day, and he strongly encouraged me to contact you. I understand that you have done extensive consulting for Fleer in the strategic planning area and that you have a number of senior-level contacts in the corporate planning functions of a number of the larger U.S. companies. Consequently, Eric seemed to feel that you might be willing to be of some assistance to me with regard to my current job search.

Dr. Aiken, I hold an MBA from Columbia University in Finance and have spent the last 25 years in the corporate planning and development field. Currently, I am Senior Vice President - Corporate Planning with Fisher Controls International, here in Baltimore.

As the result of some recent changes in senior corporate management, I have elected to confidentially explore a career change. My goal is to find a position as the senior corporate planning officer with a multi-billion dollar, high-technology company. Compensation requirements would be in the $200,000 range.

Eric suggested I contact you, thinking that perhaps you could help me make some key contacts in the industry. I am looking to identify senior-level persons, working either in or with the corporate business development function, through whom I might network in identifying an executive-level position in my field. In particular, I would like to identify individuals who are professionally very active outside their own organizations and who seem to have a number of professional contacts in the business development field. This could include corporate people, business brokers, capital venture people, key bankers, consultants, and the like.

I have enclosed a copy of my resume for your review and reference.

I will plan to call you early next week, and would greatly appreciate any thoughts that you might have on this subject.

Thank you for your help in this matter, and I look forward to speaking with you personally.

Sincerely,

Gloria A. Waldbridge

Gloria A. Waldbridge

Enclosure

KARA S. IVERSON

1701 Richards Street
Bridgeview, IL 60310

Home: (312) 398-8664
Office: (312) 227-9786

August 22, 1999

Mr. Kirk D. Foley
Regional Director
Environmental Protection Agency
7400 West 10th Street
Chicago, IL 60455

Dear Mr. Foley:

I am a recent graduate of the University of Chicago with an M.S. degree in Environmental Engineering. Although an excellent student, in view of the current economic conditions, I have been experiencing some difficulty in finding meaningful employment in my field.

In a recent conversation with Senator D'Amato, he suggested I contact you for some assistance. Senator D'Amato and my father, John Slater, were close personal friends and worked for many years on various political committees for the Democratic Party. Specifically, the Senator seemed to feel that you might be willing to help me identify expanding environmental consulting firms who may be looking for someone with my credentials.

If your schedule would permit, I would very much like to come to Chicago to discuss this matter with you directly. Perhaps you might also be kind enough to help me identify key contacts within the field. I would be most grateful for any advice and assistance that you might provide regarding this matter.

I will plan to contact you in a few days to determine if your schedule would allow us to meet. Thank you for your help, and I look forward to the possibility of meeting with you personally.

Sincerely,

Kara S. Iverson

Kara S. Iverson

Enclosure

SHERIFF PATEL
1212 Farady Avenue
Portland, ME 04112
(207) 576-9043

August 22, 1999

Ms. Jane M. Fitzpatrick
Executive Director
National Association of Consumer Affairs
200 Constitution Avenue, NW
Washington, DC 20002

Dear Jane:

Greetings from Portland, Maine! It hardly seems two years ago that we worked so hard together on the national meeting in Dallas. At least our hard work paid off, and the meeting was a major success. I don't envy you the task of having to do that each and every year. It must be exhausting.

Jane, I am writing to ask your assistance with my job search. I have decided that I would like to leave the Portland area in favor of warmer climes, and would like to center my search on the southeastern U.S. Both Atlanta and Miami would be of particular interest, however, I am quite flexible in this regard.

As you know, I have been Director of Consumer Affairs for Hanover Industries for the last three years, and have over 20 years of experience in the field. I have enclosed a complete copy of my resume for your reference. I might mention, that Hanover is totally unaware of my decision, so I would appreciate your handling this inquiry with appropriate sensitivity, which I know you will do.

In your capacity as Executive Director, I know you are contacted from time to time by companies who are looking for senior executives in the Consumer Affairs field. I would appreciate your keeping me in mind for any such inquiries.

Beyond this, however, I would like to discuss my situation with you and seek your advice regarding the best way to conduct my job search. Any thoughts and ideas you might have on this subject would be greatly appreciated. It has been quite some time since I was last in the job market.

I will plan to call you sometime next week, and hopefully will be able to catch up with you. (I recall what a busy schedule you have.) In the meantime, perhaps you will have an opportunity to review my resume.

I look forward to our conversation, Jane, and very much appreciate your assistance in this matter. Thank you.

Sincerely,

Sheriff

Sheriff Patel

Enclosure

JANICE M. REILLY
1022 Shilling Circle
Havertown, PA 19244
(713) 356-4193

April 5, 1999

Mr. Martin C. Lang
Vice President & General Counsel
Exxon Corporation
225 East John W. Carpenter
Irving, TX 75062

Dear Mr. Lang:

Jack Brier, one of my colleagues at Swan Oil, suggested that I contact you. I understand that you and Jack began your careers together at DuPont and worked together for nearly 12 years. He speaks very highly of you.

Mr. Lang, I am a corporate attorney and have worked in the Law Division of Swan Oil for two years since my graduation from Harvard Law School in 1997. My area of concentration has been Human Resources law, although I have also been exposed to both patent and antitrust law as well.

I have enclosed a copy of my resume for your reference.

My husband, Jeff, and I have arrived at a mutual decision to relocate to the Dallas area. Jeff has been offered the position of General Manager of DuPont's petrochemicals operation, and I have agreed to attempt to find a suitable position that will provide me with the opportunity for future growth and professional development.

Although you may not be aware of any openings for someone with my credentials, Jack seemed to feel that you might be willing to arrange for some personal introductions to some of your professional colleagues with other corporations in the Dallas area. As you know, it will be important for me to do extensive networking throughout the local legal community if I am going to be successful in locating a suitable career opportunity. Anything that you could do to help me in this regard will be very much appreciated.

I will be in Dallas the week beginning April 22nd to do some house hunting, and was wondering whether your schedule might allow us to get together for either lunch or dinner. I would greatly appreciate your insights concerning the Dallas legal community as well as any general suggestions you might have concerning my job search. I will give you a call to see if we can coordinate a convenient time to meet.

Jack sends his best, and wants to know when the two of you are going deep-sea fishing in the Keys again. He says he's ready whenever you are.

Thank you for your help, and I look forward to meeting with you while in Dallas.

Sincerely,

Janice M. Reilly

Janice M. Reilly

Enclosure

DOMINIC F. GALLO

217 Woodcliffe Avenue, Danbury, CT 80411   *(203) 877-9014*

November 16, 1998

Ms. Deborah R. Barnes
Senior Partner
Barnes, White & Kauffman
Attorneys at Law
23555 East Euclid Avenue
New York, NY 12201

Dear Deborah:

I really appreciated the help you gave us last year on the Coated Films Antitrust Case. The defense strategy was magnificent and the victory was sweet indeed. Obviously, we've come to have a high regard for you and your colleagues.

Deborah, I am writing to you with regard to a personal and highly confidential matter. As a result of some recent changes here at Tektronix, I have decided to quietly leave my position as General Counsel and seek a similar position with a larger company, preferably in manufacturing. I am therefore enclosing a copy of my resume for your reference.

Knowing of your excellent reputation in the field of antitrust law and some of the key national cases your firm has handled for several major U.S. companies, I thought I would contact you to see if you would be willing to be of some assistance relative to my job search. Specifically, I would appreciate the opportunity to meet with you to discuss this matter personally.

Deborah, I know that you are likely unaware of a specific opening at this time, but I would value your general observations and recommendations concerning my job search strategy, and would appreciate the opportunity to discuss this topic with you on a broader basis. I would personally find such conversation very beneficial. Perhaps we could meet over either lunch or dinner.

I will plan to call your office on Friday of this week to see when you might be available to meet. I look forward to seeing you again, and will very much appreciate your assistance on this subject.

Thank you.

Very truly yours,

Dominic Gallo

Dominic F. Gallo

DFG/tab

Enclosure

BEVERLY C. MALONE
205 Concord Road
Waterbury, CT 08506
(203) 979-0845

March 23, 1998

Mr. Sean R. Hendricks
Manager of MIS Operations
Pitney Bowes Credit Corporation
5600 Beach Tree Lane
Hartford, CT 06508

Dear Sean:

I am a close, personal friend of Maureen Sullivan, who, I understand, is a colleague of yours at Pitney Bowes. Maureen told me to contact you, feeling that you might be willing to help me with a career change that I am considering. I would be very appreciative of your assistance.

As my enclosed resume shows, I am a 1994 graduate of Columbia University with a B.S. degree in Computer and Information Science and a minor in Accounting. For the past two years, I have been employed as a Programmer/Analyst for Creative Software, a software development firm specializing in the development of computer software with applications in the human resources field. My full resume is enclosed for your reference.

I understand from Maureen, that Pitney Bowes has recently undertaken the purchase and installation of a large, broad-based human resources/payroll system. In view of my dual degree and extensive exprience with human resources sytems, perhaps I may be of some value to you.

Even if you do not have a current opening which is appropriate, I would still like to have the opportunity to meet with you. Perhaps, in exchange for some tips I might be able to pass along regarding the HR systems package you bought, you might be willing to provide me with some valuable suggestions and ideas regarding my job search. This could prove to be a mutually beneficial meeting.

I will plan to call you this Friday to see if we might be able to get together. Right now, the weeks beginning April 5th and April 12th would be convenient for me. I am quite flexible, however, and would be pleased to adjust my schedule to accommodate your needs.

Thank you for your assistance, and I look forward to the opportunity of meeting with you personally.

Sincerely,

Beverly C. Malone

Beverly C. Malone

Enclosure

2166 General Warren Blvd.
King of Prussia, PA 19406

July 23, 1999

Ms. Lynne J. Babbcock
President
J.D. Edwards & Company, Inc.
5 Technology Drive
Malvern, PA 19355

Dear Lynne:

How is the General Electric project coming along? I heard
through the grapevine that your firm had landed the multi-
million dollar installation and start-up project for GE's new
general ledger system. Congratulations, that's quite a feather
in your cap! It just goes to show that, in the long run high
quality work and talented people "can" win.

Lynne, I am writing to see if you might be willing to help me
with a personal matter. I have arrived at the conclusion that,
if I want to experience long-term career growth, I am going to
need to leave my position as MIS Development Manager at Fleming
Food Corporation. Although the company has been good to me,
capital is tight and the company is beginning to cut several
corners -- many in the MIS capital projects area.
Additionally, future growth prospects for the company look
discouraging over the next few years, as the company has lost
several of its key patent positions to competition.

I know as a consultant in the MIS field, you are well-known and
have a number of key contacts. I felt, perhaps, you might be
willing to spend a few minutes with me to review my resume and
help me with formulation of my job search strategy. Your
insights concerning current industry trends and potential
opportunity areas could be very beneficial to me at this point
in the job hunting process. I would be most appreciative if
you could share some of your observations and ideas with me.

How does your calendar look for the week beginning August 8th?
Would it be possible for you to join me for a long lunch to
discuss this matter?

I will call you in the next day or two to see if we can arrange
a convenient time to meet. As always, Lynne, I look forward to
meeting with you.

Thank you for your willingness to assist me in this matter.

                              Sincerely,

                              Edward D. Hughes

                              Edward D. Hughes

EDH:lsm

Enclosure

J. MARTIN GILLESPIE

1277 Carnation Drive
Cleveland, Ohio 44115

Home: (216) 833-5221
Office: (216) 632-8735

May 26, 1998

Mr. William D. Lynch
Regional Sales Manager
Transcon Freight Corporation
720 U.S. Highway 1
Erie, PA 17762

Dear Mr. Lynch:

As Regional Sales Manager with Transcon Freight, I am sure you are aware, from time to time, of openings in Distribution Management with some of your customers. Perhaps, one of your customers may be in the market for a young, ambitious Shipping Supervisor with strong potential for growth to senior-level management. If so, I may well be an excellent match for their requirements.

As the enclosed resume shows, I hold a B.A. degree in Logistics from the University of Cincinnati, and have slightly over two years experience as a Shipping Supervisor for Goodyear Tire & Rubber at their regional warehouse in Akron. In fact, we have been a major customer of yours and frequently use Transcon for a lot of our overnight hauls throughout the northeastern United States.

The next time you are in the Cleveland area, I would appreciate the opportunity to meet with you. As a result of your extensive contacts and knowledge of the distribution industry, it would likely be very beneficial to talk with you about my career. I would sincerely appreciate any general thoughts and/or ideas that you feel could be helpful to my career search.

I will call your office shortly, to see if your secretary could arrange such a meeting for me. This is, of course, highly confidential, since Goodyear is totally unaware of my decision.

I look forward to the prospects of meeting with you, Mr. Lynch, and would sincerely appreciate your willingness to share ideas and suggestions with me on this topic. Thank you very much.

Sincerely,

Martin Gillespie

J. Martin Gillespie

Enclosure

FRANCIS A. VANDERSLICE

2180 Barlow Road
Allentown, PA 16309

Home: (215) 533-8872
Office: (215) 741-2129

September 14, 1998

Ms. Ruth A. Glover
Director of Procurement
Lee Enterprises
111 South Calvert Street
Princeton, NJ 08906

Dear Ruth:

It was nice seeing you again at the National Association of Purchasing Agents meeting in Atlantic City this past Spring. Time has really flown, and it hardly seems like six months ago that Gene, you and I were having dinner together at Bally's. That's something we need to do more than just once a year. I have always thoroughly enjoyed our time together.

Unfortunately, Ruth, I find myself needing to face a more serious matter. Keystone Steel has just announced its decision to shut down its furnace operations in Whitehall, which means that as of November 1st I will be "on the street". I only wish they had given us a little more warning of this. With two kids currently in college, things are going to be a bit tight.

I know how active you have been over the years in NAPA, and have always admired your ability to get things done through your many personal contacts in the Association. Right now, I wish I were as well "networked" as you. It would certainly come in handy.

If your schedule would permit, I'd like to meet you for lunch sometime in the next week or so. (I'm buying!) I would really appreciate your thoughts and ideas concerning my job search strategy. It has been quite some time since I have had to look for a job, and I'm afraid that my skills are more than just a bit rusty.

As a prelude to our meeting, I am enclosing a "draft" copy of my resume and would appreciate if you could look it over. In addition, I would like to ask you to give some thought to key contacts who are well-connected in the Purchasing field. I need to begin to prepare a list of primary contacts, through whom I can network to identify an appropriate career opportunity.

I hate to dump all of this on you, but I'm really not sure where to turn at the moment. You've always been a great friend, and I know that I can count on you to help me. If you ever need help, I'm sure you already know that I will be there to lend a hand. Hopefully, you'll never need to face this one. At age 58, it's not going to be easy!

Ruth, I'll call you later this week, and we can work out the details of where and when to meet. Thanks for your help.

Best regards,

Francis A. Vanderslice

Francis A. Vanderslice

Enclosure

PATRICIA A. KAISER

2201 Laurelwood Road
Cherry Hill, NJ 08003

Home: (609) 776-8139
Office: (609) 336-5528

February 26, 1998

Mr. Clifford D. Breeding
Quality Control Manager
Sinclair Chemical Corporation
32100 Telegraph Road
Houston, TX 75082

Dear Cliff:

I have recently made a decision to leave Teledyne, Inc., where I have been a Quality Engineer for the past two years. When discussing this matter with Ben Watkins the other day, he suggested that I contact you. Ben felt you might be in a position to provide me with some good advice.

Cliff, clearly I am not expecting you will be aware of a job opportunity. Instead, I was hopeful that you might spend a few minutes with me on the phone to share any ideas you might have concerning my job search. In particular, I was hoping that you might suggest some key contacts in the quality field with whom I should be in touch as part of my job search.

Generally, the kinds of people that could prove most beneficial to know, are those who are well-connected and appear to know a number of other professionals and managers in the quality field. This might include such persons as professionals and managers working directly in the quality field, vendors who sell products and services to the quality field, consultants, key professors, etc. I would greatly appreciate if you could help me to identify such persons.

In anticipation of our conversation, I have enclosed a copy of my resume for your review and reference. I would also welcome any suggestions you might have on ways to improve the effectiveness of this document.

Anything you can do to help me with my job search effort will be greatly appreciated. Thank you very much for your help, and I look forward to talking with you.

Sincerely,

Patricia A. Kaiser

Patricia A. Kaiser

Enclosure

DAVID J. PALMER
766 West Rolling Road
Fort Washington, PA 19482
(215) 649-9144

August 22, 1998

Ms. Elaine M. Haggerty
President
The Quality Network, Inc.
6935 Arlington Road
Bethesda, MD 20814

Dear Elaine:

I am writing at the suggestion of Drew Olsen, Vice President of Quality at Nova Electronics Company, who thought perhaps you might be of assistance to me. Drew and I have known one another for several years, and are close personal friends.

During lunch with Drew yesterday, he mentioned that you had contacted him to let him know that General Electric was looking for a Director of Total Quality for their Power Products Division in Syracuse. I understand that you had been contacted by a search firm, but Drew couldn't recall which one.

Based upon what Drew has told me about this position, it would appear that I may well be a very good match for their requirements. I have both an undergraduate degree in engineering and a graduate degree in Statistics. I have spent the last 18 years in the quality field, the last four of which have been as Manager of Total Quality for IBM's Industrial Controls Division. I have enclosed a copy of my resume for your reference.

Since I would be interested in pursuing this position, I will plan to give you a call shortly. In the meantime, I would appreciate if you could confidentially pass along a copy of my resume to the search firm that contacted you.

Additionally, Elaine, I would appreciate the opportunity to talk with you more broadly about my job search. Perhaps you may have ideas on key persons with whom I should be in contact during the course of my search. I would certainly welcome any suggestions you may have on this matter.

Thank you for passing my resume along, and I look forward to speaking with you shortly.

Sincerely,

Dave Palmer

David J. Palmer

Enclosure

GAIL M. LEVINE

266 Monticello Street, Chicago, IL 60623

June 12, 1998

Mr. Leo C. Shumaker
Regional Sales Manager
Frontier Chemical Company
100 Enterprise Drive
Houston, TX 75832

Dear Leo:

I am writing to you on a confidential basis to seek your help on a personal matter. As you know, we have had some changes here at Foamex, and I am now reporting to Craig Jenkins, Vice President. I do not view this as a positive move and, as a result, I have elected to make a career change.

Although you are already somewhat familiar with my credentials, I have enclosed a copy of my resume to fill in the gaps. Highlights include a B.S. degree in Chemical Engineering and nearly four years experience in chemicals procurement. All of this has been with Foamex.

At this point in my career, I am looking for a junior-level management position in the procurement department of a major corporation, where there is the opportunity for long-term career growth. Of course, I would want to remain in the chemical process industry. Compensation requirements are in the low to mid $60,000 range, dependent upon opportunity and location.

With your large number of contacts in the procurement field in chemical process related industries, I felt that perhaps you might be aware of someone looking for a candidate with my credentials. Additionally, I would appreciate it if you could share with me the names of some key contacts in the industry, with whom it would be a good idea to touch base during the course of my job search.

When you are in the Chicago area next Wednesday, I wonder if you might have some time to spend with me on this topic. Perhaps we might have lunch or dinner together. I would also welcome your overall general advice and counsel on my job search strategy.

I recognize the potential sensitivity of this, so I want to assure you of my utmost confidentiality regarding any help which you provide. Likewise, as I'm sure you can appreciate, my decision to make a career move at this time is also a highly confidential and sensitive matter.

Leo, I will call you to see if we can work something out to meet. Thank you for helping me with this matter.

Sincerely,

Gail

Gail M. Levine

Enclosure

STEVEN E. JENNINGS
1020 Farm Springs Road
Spokane, WA 98033

October 21, 1999

Mr. Victor J. Berg
President
Chevron Chemical Company
6001 Bollinger Canyon Road
San Ramon, CA 94583

Dear Vic:

I recently heard from Janet that Bob and you went bone fishing near Catalina and had a great time. This puts me in mind of our great adventure sailfishing two years ago in Key Largo. I can't recall when I've had more fun. You always had a soft touch when it comes to going game fishing. Perhaps I could tempt you away from your work again this year to give it another try -- what do you think?

Speaking of "soft touch," I'm afraid I'm going to need your help. It seems that Chem-Trol Corporation is going to be sold to DuPont and I'm told that my position as Vice President of Procurement is to be eliminated. So, I thought I had better launch my job search sooner rather than later.

I am enclosing an advance copy of my resume, Vic, and would like to arrange to meet with you as soon as your hectic schedule will permit. I would really appreciate your advice and counsel on my job search.

I will give Sarah a call this Friday to see when we could get together. Could you please alert her to my need to meet with you?

As always, I am indebted to your generosity and look forward to our meeting. Please say "hello" to Janet for me and tell her I "send my love."

Warmest regards,

Steven E. Jennings

Steven E. Jennings

SEJ/meb

Enclosure

ERIN M. SANDERS
476 Covered Bridge Road
Newtown, PA 18970
(404) 953-2593

July 16, 1998

Mr. Peter H. Woods, Jr.
Director of Marketing
Sanyo Manufacturing Corporation
1440 Ridge Pike
Princeton, NJ 08773

Dear Pete:

You may recall that we met briefly last summer at Hal Linden's 4th of July picnic. During a recent conversation with Hal, he suggested that I contact you and reminded me of our meeting.

Pete, unfortunately, my company, Baird Electronics, has just been sold to Sony Corporation and my services as National Sales Manager are no longer required. Sony is simply folding the Baird product line into their existing sales organization which, of course, is headed by their own Director of Sales & Marketing. Friday will be my last day.

I will be in the Princeton area the week beginning July 28 and would like to meet you for lunch, should your schedule allow. I was hopeful that you might be able to share some thoughts and general advice concerning my job search. Hal says that you are quite knowledgeable of the electronics communications market and might have some general suggestions about possible job hunting strategies. I would sincerely welcome any thoughts you might have on this subject.

By way of preliminary introduction to this topic, I have enclosed a copy of my resume for your review.

I hope your schedule will allow us to get together and that you will be able to join me. I will give you a call early next week to see what your schedule looks like, and we can go from there.

Thanks for your help, and I look forward to having lunch with you.

Sincerely,

Erin Sanders

Erin M. Sanders

EMS/mag

Enclosure

ALFRED W. CHAPMAN

2206 Maple Leaf Avenue, Lancaster, PA 17762

May 16, 1998

Ms. Claire E. Spencer
Director of Corporate Accounting
Johnson Controls
8700 North Green Bay Avenue
Pttsburgh, PA 15223

Dear Claire:

The other day in a conversation with Shirley Simpson, your name came up. I was telling Shirley about my recent decision to leave my current position as General Ledger Accountant with Lancaster Labs to seek a position offering greater growth potential, when Shirley suggested that I give you a call. I understand the two of you were sorority sisters at Penn State together and still stay in close touch.

Claire, I am certainly not expecting that you will be aware of a job for me. Instead, my interest in talking with you is much broader than that. What I was hoping was that you might have a few minutes to spend with me to review my resume and provide me with some general advice regarding my current job search. I would very much value your counsel.

I will plan to call you shortly to see when might be a convenient time for us to get together. I sincerely appreciate your assistance with my job search and look forward to our discussion.

By the way, Shirley says to say "hello" and to tell you that she is planning to go to the reunion at State College in June. She will give you a call soon to see if the two of you can go together.

Thanks again for your help, and I look forward to the possibility of meeting with you.

Sincerely

Al Chapman

Alfred W. Chapman

Enclosure

MICHELLE S. GRAYBILL

330 N. Guilford Lane
Buffalo, NY 14220

Home: (716) 466-7963
Office: (716) 873-9100

October 3, 1998

Mr. Grant W. Smith
President
Omni Graphics, Inc.
1300 York Avenue
New York, NY 10221

Dear Grant:

Henry Grove and I were talking the other day, and he mentioned that you own and operate a very successful graphics arts firm that does a lot of contract work for the Elliott Lewis Agency in consumer goods advertising. As a result, Henry seemed to feel that you might be in a position to assist me, and suggested that I contact you.

Grant, until Friday of last week, I was the Creative Director for the Duckworth Advertising Agency here in Buffalo. Unfortunately, due to the sudden and unexpected death of Joseph Duckworth, the owner, his widow has elected to close the business. This leaves me in the position of seeking employment.

Rather than bore you with a lot of detail in this letter, I have decided to enclose a copy of my resume for your reference. In short, I have a Master's degree in Graphic Arts and over ten years experience on the creative side of a small family-owned consumer products advertising firm.

Henry seemed to feel that, as a result of your position and contacts in the advertising field, you might be in a position to help me with my job search. Although you may well not be aware of a specific opening, I would very much value spending an hour or so with you to get your overview of the advertising industry and some general suggestions concerning my job search strategy. I sincerely hope you will be able to meet with me.

Grant, I will plan to give you a call later this week to see if we can arrange a mutually agreeable time to meet.

Thank you for your willingness to be of help.

Very truly yours,

Michelle Graybill

Michelle S. Graybill

Enclosure

CLYDE M. SULLIVAN
10 Downing Street
New London, Connecticut 06083
(203) 847-5847

March 22, 1998

Mr. Kendall P. Harris
Senior Vice President
Aerochem, Inc.
1600 Marketplace East
Boston, MA 77046

Dear Ken:

I am a neighbor of Ed Meehan, and have known Ed for over 15 years. I understand from Ed that the two of you grew up together in the Danbury area and went on to Columbia University together. Ed suggested that I contact you, feeling that perhaps you could be of help to me.

As you are likely aware, LaRoche Chemical Corporation is preparing for another sizeable downsizing and will be offering a voluntary separation package to all of its engineering staff shortly. Since I have been with the company for over 14 years I expect to receive a fairly attractive financial package as part of this offering. I am giving serious consideration to accepting this offer and seeking career opportunities elsewhere.

Ken, I would very much appreciate the opportunity to meet with you at your convenience to get a better feel for the market. Ed tells me that you have been very active with the American Institute of Chemical Engineers over the years and have a number of key contacts in the chemical industry. Additionally, in your capacity as the head of Aerochem's' Engineering & Technology Group, Ed seemed to feel you probably have a fairly good overview of conditions and trends in the chemical industry.

Although I don't expect that you will be aware of specific jobs, I would greatly value your general advice and counsel concerning my job hunting strategy as well any relevant market information that you could provide which might impact my decision to either stay or leave LaRoche.

As a prelude to our meeting, I have taken the liberty of enclosing a copy of my resume for your reference. I will plan to call your office this Tuesday to see when it might be convenient for you to meet with me. I sincerely hope that your schedule will permit us to get together in the near future.

Thank you for your help, and I look forward to talking with you on Tuesday.

Sincerely,

Clyde Sullivan

Clyde M. Sullivan

Enclosure

MARIA A. CHAVEZ
922 Fitzwater Street
Urbana, IL 60332
(312) 967-8394

June 3, 1998

Mr. C. Benjamin Lutz
Vice President Human Resources
Titan Computer Corporation
400 East Brookline Boulevard
Chicago, IL 60603

Dear Ben:

You are no doubt aware of the current turmoil at LaserTek Computing, and the substantial losses that the company has experienced over the last two years. The continuing uncertainty of this situation has caused me to decide to seek employment opportunities elsewhere.

I have long known Ralph Fusco through the Employment Management Association and our time together on the Board and various committees. In recent conversation with Ralph, he suggested that I contact you, feeling that perhaps you could be of some help to me in my job search.

Briefly, I have an MBA from Rutgers University and eight years of Human Resources experience in the electronics industry. For the last five years, I have been Director of Employment for LaserTek Computing. A copy of my resume is enclosed for your reference.

Although you are not likely to be aware of specific job opportunities, Ben, it would be helpful if I could meet with you for an hour or so concerning my job search. I would appreciate the opportunity to discuss my job hunting strategy with you and get the benefit of your counsel concerning my approach. I would also appreciate any ideas or suggestions you might have concerning key persons within the industry with whom I should be in contact for employment networking purposes.

I will plan to contact your secretary early next week to see if your schedule will allow us to get together. I would really appreciate the opportunity to meet with you and hope that you can find some time to share some of your thoughts and ideas with me.

Thank you, and I look forward to the possibility of meeting with you in the near future.

Sincerely,

Maria A. Chavez

Maria A. Chavez

Enclosure

HARVEY B. PRICE
622 Crosby Square
Lake Moses, Washington 99144
Bus: (509) 611-2020 · Res: (509) 331-3670

June 15, 1998

Ms. Gail M. Harris
Director of Marketing
Fine Fabrics, Inc.
1135 Sussex Blvd.
Spokane, WA 99413

Dear Gail:

Last evening following our weekly tennis match, I mentioned to Frank Brady that I was considering leaving my position as National Sales Manager for Kennedy Textiles here in Spokane. Frank mentioned that he knew you quite well and strongly suggested that I give you a call. He felt, as a result of your position at Fine Fabrics, you might have some ideas or suggestions for me about my job hunting campaign.

Gail, if it wouldn't be too much of an imposition, I would really appreciate the opportunity to meet with you. Perhaps we could get together over lunch in the next week or so. I would very much value hearing your views on the state of the wholesale industry and with whom I should be in contact for networking purposes as I begin my job search.

Since you will need to know more about my background and overall qualifications, I have enclosed a copy of my resume for your reference. Your review and suggestions concerning ways in which this resume might be improved would also be very additive to my employment campaign.

I would very much appreciate the opportunity to meet with you, and hope that your schedule will allow us to get together shortly. I will call you on Thursday to check your schedule and see if we can arrange a convenient time to meet.

Gail, thank you for helping me with this matter, and I look forward to meeting you.

Sincerely,

Harvey Price

Harvey B. Price

Enclosure

6

Resume Letters

The resume letter is a cross between a cover letter and a resume. First, it is a cover letter in that it is used to transmit your credentials to the employer. Second, it is a replacement for the resume and is designed to provide a brief summary of your employment qualifications. The resume letter both transmits and sells your credentials to a prospective employer.

The popularity and use of the resume letter have grown considerably over the last few years, with more and more of these letters showing up in corporate and search firm mailboxes. The proliferation of these documents, however, is not necessarily a testimonial to their effectiveness as a job-hunting technique. There appears to be no concrete evidence that resume letters are any more effective than the conventional cover letter and resume combination.

ADVANTAGES OF RESUME LETTER

Proponents of the resume letter argue that certain advantages are realized by the job seeker in using the resume letter instead of the conventional cover letter and resume. The advantages typically cited are as follows:

1. A one-page letter format is more likely to be read than a two- or three-page letter and resume format.
2. If well written, the resume letter provides just enough information to stimulate curiosity and interest without causing the candidate to be "screened out" by the employer.
3. Providing only limited information in a resume letter can create a need for an interview. Candidates then have an opportunity to "sell" themselves—an opportunity not necessarily afforded to those sending a "complete" resume.

4. Because most managers and employment professionals receive many multipage, unsolicited resumes, one-page resume letters are appreciated.

5. Where cost is a factor, the use of a one-page resume letter can be considerably cheaper than a multipage cover letter and resume packet. The one-page approach allows the job hunter to survey a much larger employer audience for the same cost as a smaller multipage mailing.

On the surface these arguments sound good. There seems to be ample logic present to support these contentions. However, one should consider the disadvantages of the resume letter before accepting it as a job search panacea and making it the centerfold of one's job-hunting campaign.

DISADVANTAGES OF RESUME LETTER

In my opinion, most employment professionals view the resume letter with disdain. Major disadvantages cited by this group include the following:

1. Resume letters usually contain insufficient information to determine a candidate's qualifications for a given opening.

2. Lack of detailed information does not allow the employer to determine the *degree* of qualification for a given position.

3. Insufficient information does not allow a proper comparison with other qualified candidates, placing the user of the resume letter at considerable competitive disadvantage.

4. Busy employment and line managers are loath to call a candidate simply to determine whether he or she has the basic qualifications for an opening. Most will call *only* as a last resort, when there are no other qualified candidates identified. They do not wish to waste their time talking with candidates who are potentially unqualified for an open position.

5. Users of resume letters may sometimes be viewed as *suspicious* or *deceptive* by employers. Why else would they not furnish a complete accounting of their qualifications and experience in the standard resume format?

6. Some employers may view users of resume letters as *lazy*—unwilling to commit the necessary time and effort to prepare a proper resume document.

This list of disadvantages might well discourage job seekers from using the resume letter as part of their job-hunting strategy. However, there are no statistics available that measure the effectiveness of this job-search technique, so one should not write it off as worthless.

The resume letter is more effective when mailed directly to functional managers (those who have the openings) than to employment managers or personnel departments. Line managers normally receive fewer resumes and employment letters than busy human resource executives. Therefore your letter has a better chance of being read and generating a positive response.

In the final analysis, the using the resume letter in a broad-based survey campaign to functional managers at several hundred companies might be worth trying. It would be less expensive than mailing a full resume and letter packet and would allow you to reach a much larger group of employers at far less cost.

The resume letter may prove most effective in a mass mail campaign to search firms and/or employment agencies. The financial incentive (placement fees collected from client companies) is probably sufficient to motivate a search consultant to pick up a telephone and call a prospective candidate. Most search consultants are accustomed to speaking with several unqualified candidates before finding those few who will satisfy their client's needs.

COMPONENTS OF EFFECTIVE RESUME LETTER

If a resume letter is going to succeed, it must be well designed and well written. Review of the following sample resume letters will reveal certain key components that increase the effectiveness of the resume letter as a job-hunting tool. These elements are:

1. Statement of interest in employment.
2. Statement of job-search objective (position sought).
3. Broad summary of relevant qualifications, including:
   a. Educational credentials;
   b. Job-related experience;
   c. Important traits and characteristics.
4. Summary of important job-relevant accomplishments.
5. Salary and geographical requirements (optional).
6. Request for employer action.
7. Specific contact instructions (optional).
8. Statement of appreciation for consideration.

The sample resume letters provided in this chapter will assist you in creating an effective resume letter of your own. Review them carefully before deciding on the format that will best suit your specific needs.

BRIAN D. GILBERT

151 Pilgrim Avenue
Warwick, RI 02888

Home: (401) 727-9165
Office: (401) 999-0300

August 22, 1997

Mr. Vernon M. Olson
Senior Vice President
Sales & Marketing
Electronic Data Systems Corporation
330 Engineering Drive
Marietta, GA 30067

Dear Mr. Olson:

I am a highly successful National Sales Manager with an excellent, documentable record of accomplishment in the sale of electronic components to O.E.M. accounts in the defense industry. Highlights of my background include:

- B.S. and M.S. degrees in Electrical Engineering

- Direct 80 person national and international field sales force, selling direct and through distributors

- Products include microwave antennae and receiver components for military guidance and tracking systems

Key accomplishments include:

- Revamped field sales organization and market approach, driving sales from $25 million to $126 million in only four years

- Successfully introduced six new products -- all achieving sales volume which exceeded business plan objectives (2 by more than 50%)

- Reduced cost of sales by 18% over two year period

I am seeking a senior sales executive position with a high-tech electronics parts manufacturer, where there will be the opportunity to manage both the sales and marketing functions. Position could be at either the corporate or division level. My compensation requirements are a base salary of at least $125,000 plus significant incentive compensation potential based upon contribution.

If my credentials interest you, I can be reached at the numbers shown above on this letterhead. I look forward to hearing from you.

Thank you for your consideration.

Sincerely,

Brian D. Gilbert

Brian D. Gilbert

1595 Springhill Road
Overland Park, KS 66202
June 6, 1998

Mr. Richard Ferguson
President
Resource Consultants, Inc.
10 Mill Pond Lane
Overland Park, KS 66202

Dear Mr. Ferguson:

I am a talented and energetic Sales Representative with three years experience in the sale of paper converting equipment to the paper industry. My accomplishments include:

- Sales Representative of the Year, Southeast Region, 1997

- Three years of significant sales volume increase as follows:

  - 1997 → 15% increase ($100 million to $125 million)
  - 1996 → 33% increase ($ 75 million to $100 million)
  - 1995 → 25% increase ($ 60 million to $ 75 million)

- Landed company's largest single account ($12 million)

Products sold include winders, slitters, folders, wrappers, carton machines and sealing equipment. Current territory covers Oklahoma, Texas and Kansas. Sales are direct and through manufacturer representatives.

I am ready for my first sales management position, and am seeking a position at the district or regional management level with a firm offering the opportunity for advancement into senior sales management positions.

Current compensation includes a base salary of $60,000 plus bonus ($20,000 in 1997).

Please contact me, should any of your clients be looking for someone with my credentials. My home phone is (913) 877-9306. I will be pleased to furnish a complete resume at the appropriate time.

I look forward to hearing from you.

Sincerely,

Cecelia A. Bauer

Cecelia A. Bauer

CONSTANCE S. STEWARD

617 Blackhawk Drive
St. Louis, MO 63164

Home: (314) 233-9176
Office: (314) 757-2100

January 15, 1998

Mr. David C. Rafferty
Vice President Marketing
Bob Evans Farms, Inc.
3776 South High Street
Columbus, OH 43207

Dear Mr. Rafferty:

If you are currently looking for an accomplished Brand Manager with a strong consumer products background, you may want to take a look at my credentials. I have the education, experience and track record that clearly demonstrates my qualifications to play a vital role in the successful undertaking of major marketing initiatives.

My qualifications include:

- M.B.A. in Marketing, Harvard University
- Three years marketing brand management experience for a Fortune 100, consumer products company

My accomplishments include:

- Led successful introduction of major new body shampoo line achieving 15% market penetration ($300 million sales) in two years
- Successfully repositioned failing detergent line, increasing sales by 325% in three year period
- Generated highly creative advertising theme for stagnant product line, accounting for increase in market share of 28 points

I have the knowledge, creativity and drive to bring similar accomplishments to Bob Evans, given the right support and opportunity. In exchange, I am looking for the opportunity to achieve accelerated compensation and career growth commensurate with the level of my contribution to the company.

Should you wish to explore how I might help your organization to get its marketing program in high gear, I would welcome the opportunity to meet with you.

Since my search is confidential, I would appreciate it if you would contact me at my home. An answering machine will take your message and I can be back to you the following business day. Thank you for your consideration.

Sincerely,

Constance S. Steward

Constance S. Steward

YVONNE M. COUNTS
204 Hastings Avenue
Cherry Hill, NJ 08034
(609) 544-8891

October 19, 1999

Mr. Daniel C. Pearson, President
Universal Marketing Promotions
3501 Frontage Road
Tampa, FL 33607

Dear Mr. Pearson:

I am seeking an equity position as a Partner in a small to medium-sized marketing consulting firm. I have strong credentials and can bring the Fortune 100 marketing perspective to an emerging consulting practice.

Consider the following credentials:

- M.B.A. in Marketing, University of Southern California

- 25 years Marketing experience as follows:

  - 5 years, Vice President Marketing, Clorox Corporation
  - 3 years, Director of Marketing, Scott Paper Company
  - 5 years, Senior Brand Manager, Campbell Soup Company
  - 3 years, Brand Manager, Campbell Soup Company
  - 2 years, Brand Manager, Kraft Foods
  - 2 years, Associate Brand Manager, Kraft Foods
  - 3 years, Senior Marketing Analyst, Kraft Foods
  - 2 years, Market Research Analyst, Kraft Foods

My years of experience are replete with marketing success stories, with major contributions easily documented in all marketing categories from new product introductions to brand repositioning, through successful national roll-out of numerous product lines.

At this stage in my career, I would like to step back from the corporate political environment and once again focus my energies on the technical side of Marketing. I have considerable experience and numerous contacts that could well benefit a growing consulting firm that is looking to penetrate the major consumer product companies.

If what I have told you is of interest, let me suggest we meet to further explore the strengths that I could bring to your firm. Confidential calls can be placed to my office at the number shown above. I look forward to hearing from you and thank you for your consideration.

Sincerely,

Yvonne M Counts

Yvonne M. Counts

DIANE M. LOUGHERTY
1046B Golden Drive
Hunt Valley, MD 21031
(410) 996-297

January 20, 1999

Mr. Michael Pittman
Operations Manager
Packaging Corporation of America
1255 Avenue of the Americas
Evanston, IL 60204

Dear Mr. Pittman:

I am a young, ambitious project engineer looking for an opportunity to break into operations management. Specifically, I am looking for a position as a Shift Supervisor or Department Manager in a papermaking or converting operation, where I can put my technical knowledge and leadership skills to work.

The following is a short synopsis of my credentials:

- B.S., Mechanical Engineering, Bucknell University
- One year as Senior Project Engineer - Papermaking
- Two years as Project Engineer - Converting

I have strong interpersonal and leadership skills. These have been clearly demonstrated through my on-campus activities while at Bucknell. Evidence of these skills includes:

- Sorority President, Senior Year
- Sorority Vice President, Junior Year
- Sorority Pledge Master, Sophomore Year
- Captain, Women's Varsity Swim Team, Senior Year
- President, American Society of Mechanical Engineers

I am now ready to make my career transition from technical support to line manufacturing management. With my combination of strong technical and leadership skills, coupled with considerable energy and enthusiasm, I feel my new employers will experience an outstanding return on their investment.

I hope you have heard enough to stimulate your interest and that I will be hearing from you shortly. Thank you for your consideration.

Very truly yours,

Diane M. Lougherty

Diane M. Lougherty

CATHERINE L. ALBRECHT

455 Creekside Drive, Cincinnati, Ohio 45233

August 25, 1998

Mr. Bernard V. McDonald
Vice President, Operations
Scott Paper Company
Scott Plaza
Philadelphia, PA 19113

Dear Mr. McDonald:

I am currently employed in Operations Management with one of your key competitors, Procter & Gamble, and have decided to make a career change. I am seeking a senior-level operations management position at the division or corporate level, with multi-plant P&L responsibility.

In my current position as General Manager of P&G's Cincinnati Plant, I am responsible for overall management of a 1,500-employee papermaking and converting facility involved in the manufacture of sanitary tissue and household paper products. This mill includes four twin-wire Yankee tissue machines and full converting facilities.

Educationally, my qualifications include a B.S. degree in Mechanical Engineering from the University of Wisconsin and an M.B.A. from Duke. I have had considerable management training while with P&G, including several courses related to the development and utilization of "high performance work teams." Additionally, I have been thoroughly schooled in modern manufacturing systems and concepts including SPC-based total quality, MRP, JIT, etc.

My experience at P&G has prepared me well to assume senior-level management responsibilities in a major pulp and paper company. During my 15 years with the company, I have advanced through a series of functional assignments including engineering, engineering management, human resources management, distribution management and operations management. I have held key operations management positions in both papermaking and converting.

Throughout my career, I have continuously maintained the highest possible performance ratings, and my operations have always rated in the top 10% in operation efficiencies within the Paper Division. During the last two years, the Cincinnati Plant, for example, has been rated the best overall performing plant site and has received P&G's coveted "Plant of the Year" award.

Mr. McDonald, should you have a need for a senior-level manufacturing executive with a strong record of achievement in the manufacture of consumer paper products, I would welcome the opportunity to meet with you. I can be reached during evening hours at my home phone, (216) 949-1593.

Thank you for your consideration.

Sincerely,

Catherine L. Albrecht

Catherine L. Albrecht

DONALD P. SHUSTER
210 Robindale Road
Irving, TX 75015

October 15, 1997

Mr. Thomas F. Connolly
Engineering Manager
Strawbridge Lithography
750 Technology Drive
Irving, TX 75015

Dear Mr. Connolly:

I am a young, hard-working Control Systems Engineer with two years plant project engineering experience in the design, installation and start-up of computer control systems on high-speed web handling equipment. My background and experience would appear to be well-suited to your web product manufacturing processes.

Highlights of my qualifications include:

- B.S. Degree, Systems Engineering, University of Wisconsin

- Two years, Control Systems Engineering, Kimberly-Clark Corporation, Neenah Plant

- Engineering design, installation, start-up of $5 million TDC 3000 Control System Project (Paper Machine and Converting Equipment)

  Project included engineering of complete system -- computers, instrumentation and related control devices

I am seeking a position at the senior project engineering or supervisory level in the control systems area. My compensation requirements are in the high $40K range.

Should you be in the market for a strong control systems professional or manager, I would welcome the opportunity to meet with you. I can be reached at my office on a confidential basis during business hours. My office phone is (214) 838-9773.

Thank you for your consideration and I look forward to hearing from you.

Sincerely,

Donald P. Shuster

Donald P. Shuster

480 Belmont Avenue
Bedminster, NJ 07921

March 29, 1999

Dr. Bruce D. Fuller
Vice President, Engineering
Magnavox Industrial Electronics Corporation
2525 Production Road
Fort Wayne, IN 46808

Dear Dr. Fuller:

If you are in search of a senior-level engineering executive to manage your company's central engineering department, you may want to give serious consideration to my candidacy.

Highlights of my qualifications include:

- M.S., Electrical Engineering, M.I.T.

- B.S., Mechanical Engineering, M.I.T.

- M.B.A., Finance, Stanford University

- 25 years Engineering/Engineering Management experience as follows:

    - 5 years, Vice President Engineering, Ford Aerospace
    - 4 years, Director of Engineering, Ford Aerospace
    - 6 years, Manager, Corporate Engineering, Hughes Aircraft
    - 4 years, Department Manager, Mechanical Design, Hughes Aircraft
    - 6 years, Engineer/Senior Project Engineer, Boeing Corporation

In my current position as Vice President of Engineering for Ford Aerospace, I manage a 600 employee central engineering group responsible for all capital project work throughout the company. This includes engineering and start-up of complete manufacturing plants, installation of new manufacturing lines in existing facilities and major rebuild work. Annual capital budget is in the $1 to $1.5 billion range.

I have established an excellent reputation for the quality and quantity of capital project work completed by my organization and have a strong reputation as both a demanding and fair leader. Most of the engineering project work performed under my direction has come in at or below budget, and I enjoy an excellent reputation for meeting key project deadlines.

My decision to leave Ford is a confidential one, and the company is totally unaware of my present job search. Current compensation is in the high $100K range.

Should you have an interest in my credentials, I would be pleased to meet with you to explore the contributions that I could make to your engineering efforts. My home phone number is (908) 494-3304. Thank you.

Sincerely,

Thomas E. Holloway

Thomas E. Holloway

CHARLENE F. SCHROEDER, Ph.D.

5110 Rutherford Road
New Britain, CT 06051

Home: (203) 436-6267
Office: (203) 827-3200

October 22, 1998

Dr. Richard E. Scott
Research Director
Department of Virology
Wyeth-Ayerst Laboratories
P.O. Box 8299
Philadelphia, PA 19101

Dear Dr. Scott:

I am a Research Investigator with over ten years experience in antiviral related research. I am very much aware of the work that your department is doing in this area, and would be interested in exploring opportunities as a member of your research staff.

My credentials include a Ph.D. in Molecular Biology from the University of Pennsylvania, where I spent six years in a post-doctoral program doing basic research related to virology. Since then I have been employed as a research scientist in the Antiviral Department of Merck & Company, Inc., where I have conducted independent research studies to define unique viral targets for antiviral intervention and have collaborated with other research groups in the design and development of novel antiviral agents.

The basic research budget at Merck has recently been cut, and several of my research projects have been adversely affected. Consequently, I am looking for a company that has a strong commitment to its basic research programs and is heavily funding projects in the antiviral area. Wyeth-Ayerst appears to fit these criteria rather well.

My current annual compensation is $68,000, and I would require an offer in the mid $70,000 range in order to give serious consideration to making a career move.

Should you have an interest in my credentials, Dr. Scott, I would welcome the opportunity to meet with you to explore how I might contribute to your research programs and objectives. I can be reached at my home during the evening or, on a confidential basis, at my office during the day.

Thank you for considering me and I look forward to hearing from you.

Very truly yours,

Charlene F. Schroeder

Charlene F. Schroeder

JOHN A. HALBROOK

9341 Courtland Drive
Richmond, VA 23219

Home: (804) 232-9439
Office: (804) 767-8310

April 21, 1998

Mr. Vincent P. Benedict
Vice President, Research & Development
Hercules Inc.
Hercules Plaza
Wilmington, DE 19898

Dear Mr. Benedict:

I recently heard a rumor that you might be looking for a Director of Research Laboratories at your corporate offices in Wilmington. If this is true, I wanted to let you know of my strong interest in this position.

As Vice President of Technology for BioSci Industries, I direct all research activities of a 110 employee research center engaged in biotechnology research. During my five years in this capacity, we have developed and successfully launched over 20 new products, accounting for a dramatic increase in annual sales volume ($75 million to $220 million). Additionally, we currently have over 50 key patents pending, which could more than double current sales in less than two years.

Educationally, I hold a Ph.D. in Biochemistry from the University of Southern California and an M.B.A. in Finance & Marketing from Pepperdine University. I have over 20 years experience in biotechnology research having started as a Research Scientist and advanced through several professional and managerial assignments to my current position.

I am a strong team player, and have developed an excellent reputation for working closely with the marketing and manufacturing functions to rapidly develop and successfully commercialize a number of new products. My interpersonal and communications skills are excellent.

I have long admired the work that Hercules has been doing in the field of cancer and virology research and would welcome the opportunity to join your senior management team as Director of your research effort.

Should you be interested in pursuing my candidacy, I would be pleased to meet with you at your convenience. I can be reached at the phone numbers shown on the above letterhead.

Thank you for your consideration.

Sincerely,

John A. Halbrook

John A. Halbrook

WILLIAM D. SINCLAIR

621 South Lennon Avenue
Boston, MA 02134

Home: (617) 591-7806
Office: (617) 228-8484

June 23, 1998

Ms. Margaret Morales
Director of Corporate Accounting
Microdyne Corporation
3601 Eisenhower Avenue
Alexandria, VA 22304

Dear Ms. Morales:

If you are looking for a strong General Ledger Accountant for either a corporate or division-level assignment, you may want to consider giving me a call.

I hold a B.S. degree in Accounting from the University of Indiana and have had four years accounting experience with the Northwestern Insurance Company. Previous experience includes two years as an Auditor with Price Waterhouse, during which time I received my C.P.A.

Currently, I am a Senior Accountant in Northwestern's Corporate Accounting Department. In this capacity I report to the Manager of Corporate Accounting and have functional accountability for reconciliation of general ledger account balances, preparation of monthly profit and loss statements, compliance with external filing requirements and related financial analyses.

I am thoroughly familiar with all aspects of general ledger accounting and associated standard accounting procedures. I am also well-versed in both federal and state filing requirements and work closely with the Corporate Tax Department in preparation of federal, state and local tax returns.

As you may be aware, Northwestern has recently undertaken a massive downsizing effort, reducing the size of its corporate staff by nearly 35%. My position is only one of several hundred positions that the company has elected to eliminate.

If you are looking for someone with my credentials, or if you are aware of any openings outside of Microdyne, I would appreciate hearing from you.

Thank you for your time and consideration.

Sincerely,

William D. Sinclair

William D. Sinclair

Marilyn M. Stewart
680 Wilshire Boulevard
Santa Ana, CA 92704
(714) 828-3166

September 16, 1999

Mr. David C. Busch
Chief Financial Officer
Rubbermaid Incorporated
1147 Akron Road
Wooster, OH 44691

Dear Mr. Busch:

I have recently decided to make a career change and am currently looking for a senior accounting management position at the director or vice presidential level with a major consumer products company. The position I seek could be at either the corporate or division level.

Should you be in the market for a strong accounting executive for a key management position at Rubbermaid, you may want to consider my credentials as follow:

- MBA, Finance, Columbia University
- BS, Accounting, Rutgers University
- CPA, Commonwealth of Pennsylvania

- Key Accounting Management experience includes:

  - 3 years, Division Controller, Johnson & Johnson
  - 2 years, Director Corporate Accounting, Johnson & Johnson
  - 3 years, Manager Corporate Accounting, Johnson & Johnson
  - 2 years, Tax Manager, Campbell Soup
  - 2 years, Auditing Manager, Campbell Soup
  - 3 years, Plant Accountant, Campbell Soup
  - 2 years, Senior Manufacturing Accountant, Campbell Soup
  - 1 year, Manufacturing Cost Accountant, Campbell Soup
  - 2 years, Auditor, Coopers & Lybrand

My rapid advancement and career progression should provide solid evidence that I have been a strong performer throughout my professional career. Additionally, I have been continuously categorized by those to whom I have reported as a charismatic leader with excellent interpersonal and communication skills.

Should this brief summary of my qualifications be of interest to you, I would be very happy to meet with you personally to explore opportunities with your company. I sincerely appreciate your consideration and look forward to your reply.

Sincerely,

Marilyn M. Stewart

Marilyn M. Stewart

JACQUELINE M. HARTLEY
9 Foothill Lane
Redmond, WA 98052

April 12, 1998

Mr. Roy H. Stahl
Director of Corporate Finance
Philip Morris Companies, Inc.
120 Park Avenue
New York, NY 10017

Dear Mr. Stahl:

If you are looking to add a young, experienced Financial Analyst to your staff with a strong background in merger and acquisition analysis, you may want to take a close look at my credentials. I have the education and experience that could prove very beneficial to your M&A program.

Please consider the following credentials:

- MBA in Finance, Amos Tuck School, Dartmouth

- BS in Chemical Engineering, Princeton University

- Four years experience in merger and acquisition analysis - Standard Brands Company, Corporate Development Department.

Key accomplishments include:

- Analysis of 16 acquisition candidates

- Development of acquisition analysis computer model allowing department to double productivity

- Recommendations resulted in purchase of four companies, all of which have met or exceeded ROI expectations.

If my qualifications interest you, I would appreciate the opportunity to meet with you to further explore my capabilities and the contributions I could make to Philip Morris.

I can be reached at my office (Phone: 206-477-3909) during the day or at my home (Phone: 206-828-4392) during evening hours. Thank you for your consideration.

Sincerely,

Jacqueline M. Hartley

Jacqueline M. Hartley

JULIA A. ABBOTT
960 Wellington Court
Tulsa, OK 74103

(918) 583-6493

April 4, 1998

Mr. Keith A. Sheffield
President
Sheffield Consulting Group
310 Pleasant Avenue
Chicago, IL 60606

Dear Mr. Sheffield:

Should you be conducting a search for someone with my strong management experience, I would be interested in discussing with you how my abilities may match your clients' needs.

My last position as Vice President of Direct Phone Operations at Vandcourt Investments gave me the opportunity to expand on many years' consulting in the design and implementation of financial and business planning processes. My MBA in Finance from the University of Chicago Business School proved to be a firm foundation upon which to build.

The remainder of my experience has been split between operations and business planning. My undergraduate training in engineering has provided me with the analytical and problem-solving skills to quickly identify critical factors underlying business performance, and design and implement the programs required to improve operations significantly. Over 70% of my experience has involved international operations.

I am seeking a senior finance or business development role with a small to medium-sized company. Target industries include petrochemical, chemical, biotech, high tech, transportation and specialty materials.

My qualifications and experience are strongly multi-functional, giving me the managerial breadth to add considerable value to my employer, especially in dynamic growth or turnaround environments. I would like to talk with you in more detail about the contributions and value I could bring to your clients. I will call you shortly to accomplish this.

Sincerely,

Julia A. Abbott

Julia A. Abbott

18 Fox Lane
Broomall, PA 19008

September 28, 1999

Mr. Francis L. Butler
Director of Corporate Planning
Shell Oil Company
Two Shell Plaza
P.O. Box 1499
Houston, TX 77252

Dear Mr. Butler:

As a Corporate Planning Manager for a major oil and petrochemical company, perhaps you are looking for a talented and accomplished analyst to join your staff. As a Senior Planning Analyst for one of Shell's key competitors, my background could be of particular interest to you.

My overall qualifications include an MBA in Finance from Texas A&M and four years experience in the Corporate Planning Department of ARCO Chemical Company, where I have worked as both a Planning Analyst and Senior Planning Analyst. Key projects on which I have worked have included:

- Analysis and long-range forecast of business growth potential for Lubricants Division

- Study and recommendations concerning feasibility of entering the mass retail market for motor oils

- Economic feasibility study and recommendations on proposed multi-million dollar expansion of the Philadelphia Refinery

- Numerous "what if" studies to support Executive Committee in preparation of corporate long-range strategic plans

I have consistently achieved high performance evaluations and am recognized as one of the top contributors within the planning department. Additionally, I have frequently been assigned as the Lead Senior Analyst on most of the company's key planning projects.

Should you wish to discuss my qualifications further, I can be reached at (610) 353-9144 during the day or (610) 559-3176 during the evening.

I appreciate your consideration and look forward to the prospect of hearing from you.

Sincerely,

David A. Low

David A. Low

RAYMOND J. LEAHY

306 Friendship Lane
Evanston, IL 60204

Home: (708) 399-7149
Office: (708) 687-4210

July 31, 1998

Mr. Robert T. Porterfield
Executive Vice President
Federal Paperboard Company, Inc.
2208 North Pearl Street
Bolton, NC 28423

Dear Mr. Porterfield:

I have been watching the rapid growth of Federal Paperboard over the last five years and have been quite impressed with the company's strategic leadership. Your careful positioning in the value-added segment of the market has done much to move you far ahead of the competition. Your record has been most impressive!

Two years ago, I left my position as Director of Corporate Planning with Packaging Corporation of America to accept the position of Vice President of Corporate Planning with Transamerica Corporation. Although I have done well in this assignment, I miss the excitement of working for a manufacturing company. Consequently, I have decided to return to the packaging industry and am seeking a senior-level position in corporate planning.

My credentials include an MBA in Finance from Stanford University and over 18 years experience in corporate planning and finance. Most of my career has been with PCA, where I advanced rapidly through a series of financial and planning assignments. This included two years as Director of Corporate Finance and nearly four years as Director of Corporate Planning.

Some of my key accomplishments at PCA have included:

- Successful acquisition of six corrugated mills, doubling the company's corrugated manufacturing capacity.

- Led company's entry into the laminated bleached board market, now the most profitable segment of the business (62% of net profits).

- Sale of company's Folding Box Division to Champion International Corporation for $960 million (considered a major strategic coup).

Perhaps you may be looking for a strong executive to head your planning function. If so, I would welcome the opportunity to meet with you to further explore my qualifications and to discuss the possible contribution I could make to your company.

Thank you for your consideration.

Sincerely,

Raymond J. Leahy

Raymond J. Leahy

MITCHELL D. LIVINGSTON

2301 Preston Park Blvd., 3A
Rockville, Maryland 21201

Home: (301) 937-4706
Office: (301) 543-0900

March 15, 1997

Mr. Walter F. Bain
Bain & Company, Inc.
1700 Constitution Blvd.
Washington, DC 20003

Dear Mr. Bain:

As key lobbyists for the tobacco industry, you could well have some interest in my background as a Legislative Affairs Specialist for your firm. Please consider my credentials.

I am a 1993 graduate from the University of Maryland with a Master's degree in Government & Politics. For the past two years, I have been employed as a Legislative Representative for the National Tobacco Manufacturer's Association at their national offices in Washington. In this position, I am responsible for representing the interests of the Association with respect to pending legislative matters and working with coalitions of various lobbying interests to influence legislation having impact on the industry.

Some of my key accomplishments have included the following:

- Was the key catalyst in combining the efforts of 12 different associations and lobbying firms to defeat the *No Smoking on Public Conveyance Bill*.

- Worked with top aides of Senator Harrison's office to re-word the Clean Air Act to minimize its negative effect on the Tobacco Industry.

Prior to this, I worked for two years as a Legislative Assistant to Senator John Thornton. In this capacity, I was heavily involved in researching and drafting key legislation which the Senator wished to support. In addition, I worked behind the scenes to solicit senatorial support and align a variety of political forces in support of sponsored legislation.

I feel my political connections, coupled with my knowledge of the inner workings of the political system, could prove quite valuable to a lobbying consulting firm such as yours.

Should you agree, I would welcome the opportunity to meet with you to explore how I might fit into your organization. Thank you for your consideration and I look forward to hearing from you.

Sincerely,

Mitchell D. Livingston

Mitchell D. Livingston

WILLIAM P. DIETZ

118 Harding Drive
Villanova, PA 19087

Home: (610) 337-5276
Office: (610) 878-3304

October 28, 1998

Ms. Evelyn Silber, President
Career Search, Inc.
1840 Century Park East
Los Angeles,CA 90067

Dear Ms. Silber:

I did not wish to bore you by sending yet another unsolicited resume to your attention. Instead, this letter will serve to briefly highlight my credentials so that you can ascertain the appropriateness of my qualifications for current search assignments on which you may now be working.

I hold an M.A. in English (communications emphasis) from Northwestern University and have over 20 years experience in the field of Public Affairs. A brief summary of recent experience follows:

- 5 years - Vice President Public Affairs, Commodore Computers
- 3 years - Director of Communications, Franklin Mint
- 4 years - Manager Employee Communications, DuPont Company

The current economic turmoil at Commodore, coupled with the frequent changes of company president, have prompted my decision to seek employment in a more stable environment.

I am seeking a senior executive-level position in Public Affairs in a medium-sized or major corporation, which has demonstrated a solid record of growth and financial performance. My compensation requirements are in the $125,000 to $135,000 range, and I am open to geographic relocation.

Should you have a client who has a need for a seasoned Public Affairs executive, I would welcome your call. Should our conversation lead to continued interest, I would be pleased to furnish you with a complete copy of my resume at that time.

Thank you for considering my qualifications and I look forward to hearing from you should you have an appropriate assignment that fits my background and interests.

Sincerely,

William P. Dietz

William P. Dietz

DEBORAH L. ALTIERI
1717 Avondale Terrace
West Chester, PA 19382

September 21, 1997

Mr. Martin C. Fox, Esq.
Fox Rothchild O'Brien & Frankel
Attorneys at Law
9226 South Orange Street
Media, PA 19063

Dear Mr. Fox:

A recent graduate of the University of Pennsylvania School of Law with over four years previous experience as a Law Clerk for the corporate legal department of Campbell Soup Company, I am ready for my first assignment as a practicing attorney. Please consider my credentials as follow:

- J.D., University of Pennsylvania School of Law (with Honors)

- B.S., Political Science, University of Pennsylvania (*cum laude*)

- Four years, Law Clerk, Campbell Soup Company

During my employment with Campbell Soup, I worked in two areas of law. Three of these years were spent doing patent research and handling a portion of the patent filing process under the direction of Martin H. Sweeney, Corporate Patent Attorney. The remaining year was spent providing research and support to William Kursner in the area of consumer litigation.

My educational background and work experience with Campbell Soup have provided me with a solid foundation upon which to build a successful career in the practice of law. I would like to begin my career with a private law practice such as yours where, through hard work and contribution to the firm, I might eventually have the opportunity to advance to the position of Partner.

Should you be looking for a well-educated, ambitious young attorney to join your firm, I would welcome the opportunity to meet with you to explore this possibility. With my drive and motivation to succeed, I know that I can make a substantive contribution to the firm.

My home telephone number is (610) 431-2237. Thank you for your consideration and I look forward to hearing from you.

Sincerely,

Deborah L. Altieri

Deborah L. Altieri

ERNEST GIBBS

766 Providence Road
Buffalo, NY 10577

March 26, 1998

Ms. Nanci Raphael
President
The Raphael Group
420 Granite Run Corporate Center
Princeton, NJ 08989

Dear Ms. Raphael:

Should one of your client corporations be searching for a Vice President and General Counsel, you may want to consider my credentials. Some highlights of my qualifications are:

*   LL.B., University of Virginia, School of Law.

*   Direct 25 person corporate law department for $15 billion electronic components manufacturer.

*   Over 20 years corporate law experience with major corporations.

In my current position as General Counsel for Franklin Electronics, I report to the President and am responsible for all legal matters pertaining to the operation of this $16 billion corporation. Some of my major achievements include:

*   Settlement of a $120 million government contract law suit for $18 million on an out-of-court basis.

*   Won major antitrust case which would have required divestiture of most profitable division.

*   Defeated major class action suit that would have cost government contracts valued at $85 million.

My current annual compensation if $145,000 ($120,000 base salary plus $25,000 executive bonus). I qualify for stock options and am provided with a company car.

Should you feel one of your clients may have an interest in my background, I would welcome the opportunity to talk with you. I can be reached at my office, phone (516) 991-8507.

Thank you.

Sincerely,

Ernest Gibbs

Ernest Gibbs

SCOTT D. CALLAHAN

1541 East Shelbyville Road, Wilmington, DE 19898

June 22, 1998

Mr. Walter D. Kincannon
MIS Manager
Midlantic Corporation
155 Howell Avenue
Baltimore, MD 21776

Dear Mr. Kincannon:

I recently learned that you are installing a Novello System 200 at your corporate offices in Minneapolis. I have been Project Manager for the successful installation and start-up of this same system at MBNA Corporation here in Wilmington, and could be a valuable asset to your project.

Some highlights of my career include:

- B.S., Computer Science, University of Washington

- Five years MIS experience with MBNA as follows:

  - 1 year - Project Manager, Novello System 200
  - 2 years - Senior Analyst, Human Resource Systems
  - 1 year - Analyst, Accounting Systems
  - 1 year - Programmer/Analyst General Support

For your general information, Novello System 200 poses a particular challenge since certain key documentation is missing. Additionally, some of the functionality which Novello lists in its product specification is simply nonfunctional and needs debugging.

If you are interested in hiring an experienced Novello System 200 Project Leader who has been on the "bleeding edge of technology," you may want to give me a call. I can probably save you many weeks of installation time and a lot of stress and frustration.

Should you wish to contact me, I can be reached at (302) 868-7419. Thank you for your consideration.

Sincerely,

Scott D. Callahan

Scott D. Callahan

DEAN R. SUMMERS
1032 King's Castle Drive
Melbourne, FL 32901

June 16, 1998

Mr. Peter J. Elkhart
Senior Vice President
Corporate Administration
Logicon, Inc.
2100 Washington Boulevard
Arlington, VA 22204

Dear Mr. Elkhart:

Some recent management changes at Rockwell International have prompted my decision to seek a career change. This decision is highly confidential, and senior management is unaware of my intention. I am seeking a senior, executive-level position in MIS management with a major, high-technology manufacturer.

Highlights of my qualifications are as follow:

- MBA, University of Connecticut

- B.S., Computer Science, Georgia Tech

- 26 years MIS experience with most recent career assignments as follow:

  - 5 years - Vice President, MIS, Rockwell International
  - 2 years - Director of MIS, Rockwell International
  - 2 years - Manager MIS Operation, IBM Corporation
  - 1 year - Manager Client Services, IBM Corporation

In my current position as Vice President MIS at Rockwell, I report to the Executive Vice President - Administration, and have responsibility for directing a 240-person MIS function with operating and administrative budget of $43 million. Some key accomplishments include:

- Successful installation and start-up of $20 million, corporate-wide general ledger system.

- Successful installation and start-up of $18 million, corporate-wide, totally integrated order entry and tracking/production and inventory scheduling/purchasing system.

I have enjoyed an excellent reputation for timely delivery of state-of-the-art MIS systems that have greatly improved management decision-making efficiency and company productivity at highly competitive costs. Excellent references are readily available.

Should you have an interest in my qualifications. I can be reached at (407) 768-3306. Thank you for your consideration.

Sincerely,

Dean R. Summers

Dean R. Summers

JAMES P. HAYWOOD
219 Sugartown Road
Rosemont, Pennsylvania 19344

September 14, 1998

Mr. Dennis T. Avery
Manager of Distribution
SmithKline Beecham
Broad & Chestnut Streets
Philadelphia, PA 19101

Dear Mr. Avery:

I recently read about SmithKline's plan to construct a 900,000 square foot manufacturing and distribution facility in Montgomery County. This suggests that you may shortly be in need of experienced distribution professionals. If so, please consider my qualifications as follows:

- B.A., Business Administration, Temple University

- Four years' distribution center management experience as follows:

    - 1 year   - Distribution Center Manager
                 Campbell Soup Company, Camden, NJ

    - 2 years - Warehouse Supervisor
                 Campbell Soup Company, Camden, NJ

    - 1 year   - Shipping Expeditor
                 Campbell Soup Company, Camden, NJ

Some key contributions have included:

- Conducted one-year carrier study, resulting in major shift from truck to rail shipments (18% annual cost savings).

- Improved production efficiency by 12% and decreased product damage by 65% through reconfiguration of high-volume product storage pattern to reduce product handling.

I have been watching SmithKline's impressive growth and would very much like to have the chance to explore employment opportunities with your firm. I am hopeful, therefore, that I will be hearing from you.

I can be reached at (610) 527-3615. Thank you for your consideration.

Sincerely,

James P. Haywood

James P. Haywood

322 Drummers Lane
White Plains, NY 80776

August 21, 1998

Mr. Theodore W. Graske
Executive Vice President
Richardson Foods Corporation
3076 Kesslinger Road
Ridgewood, NY 11385

Dear Mr. Graske:

If you are in search of a strong candidate for a senior-level Logistics management position with your corporate staff or one of your larger divisions, you may want to take a moment to consider my credentials. My background in the consumer goods industry, coupled with significant contributions in the Logistics area, may well be of interest to you.

Currently Corporate Director of Logistics for Lever Brothers, I direct a staff of 65 employees responsible for management of all Logistics activities for this $2.8 billion dollar consumer goods manufacturer on a worldwide basis. Functional responsibility includes: production planning and scheduling, purchasing, scheduling and management of raw materials inventories and warehousing and distribution management.

My credentials include a Master's degree in Distribution Management from the University of Tennessee and a B.S. degree in Industrial Engineering from Purdue University. I have 22 years' experience in Logistics and Logistics management at two major companies (Lever Brothers and Pope & Talbot), and have held a series of progressively responsible management positions in most functional areas which comprise the Logistics area.

I have had a strong history of being a key contributor to overall business strategy, and have implemented numerous programs resulting in millions of dollars of savings to my employers. I also enjoy an excellent reputation as a manager and leader of people. Interpersonal and communication skills are strong points as well.

I would appreciate the opportunity to meet with you and other appropriate members of your senior management team to explore how I might fit into your organization, and to discuss the potential contributions I could make to your company. Should you wish to explore this matter, I can be reached at (516) 247-2155.

Thank you for your consideration.

Sincerely,

Michael J. Faye

MARY ANNE CIZYNSKI

611 Strawberry Hill Road
Concord, MA 01742

Home: (617) 497-8728
Office: (617) 310-6776

November 21, 1998

Mr. James H. Keyes
Director of Quality
Johnson & Johnson Consumer Products, Inc.
Grandview Road
Skillman, NJ 08558

Dear Mr. Keyes:

If you are currently in the market for an outstanding candidate for a Quality management position at Johnson & Johnson, you will likely have an interest in my qualifications. Please consider the following credentials:

- B.S. Degree, Industrial Engineering, University of Massachusetts

- Certified Quality Engineer, A.S.Q.C., 1995

- Regional Chairperson, A.S.Q.C., Northeast Region (two years)

- Total Quality Education:

  - Dr. G. Edwards Deming Seminar, 1994
  - Crosby Quality College Graduate, 1993
  - Statistical Process Control, University of Tennessee, 1992
  - Introduction to Quality Statistics, 1992

- Six years Quality Management experience with The Gillette Company as follows:

  - 2 years - Quality Manager, Framingham Plant
  - 2 years - Assistant Quality Manager, Corporate Offices
  - 2 years - Quality Associate, Corporate Offices

I have a strong background in the design and implementation of SPC-based total quality initiatives in chemical process manufacturing facilities, and am up-to-date with most leading-edge quality concepts and approaches. My knowledge and leadership have earned me solid recognition at Gillette as well as external recognition by A.S.Q.C., where I now serve as Chairperson for the Northeast Region.

Should you have an interest in my background and wish to further explore my possible candidacy, I can be reached at the phone numbers shown above. Thank you for your consideration.

Sincerely,

Mary Anne Cizynski

Mary Anne Cizynski

DONNA F. DOYLE

801 Centerview Parkway, Milwaukee, WI 53669

October 4, 1997

Mr. Douglas T. Werner
Vice President of Operations
West Bend Company
400 Washington Street
West Bend, WI 53095

Dear Mr. Werner:

I am a well-seasoned, knowledgeable Quality executive with a strong background in the metals industry. I am seeking a position at the Director or Vice President level with a progressive metals industry manufacturer that is looking for strong leadership in the corporate-wide implementation of a total quality initiative.

Please consider my credentials:

- B.S. Degree, Mechanical Engineering, Penn State University

- Certified Quality Engineer, American Society of Quality Control

- 16 years experience in the quality field, which includes:

    - 4 years - Director of Quality, Speed Queen Company
    - 5 years - Manager of Quality, Speed Queen Company
    - 2 years - Quality Supervisor, Rayovac Corporation
    - 1 year - Senior Quality Engineer, Rayovac Corporation
    - 3 years - Quality Engineer, Rayovac Corporation

In my current position as Director of Quality at Speed Queen, I have led the design and implementation of a highly successful SPC-based total quality program on a corporate-wide basis. This included the corporate staff and the company's three manufacturing facilities. The program has cut customer complaints by 92% and reduced scrap by more than 80%. Estimated annual savings of this major initiative is in the $15 to $20 million range.

Should you have an interest in my qualifications, please feel free to contact me at my office, (414) 234-6026.

Thank you for your consideration and I look forward to hearing from you.

Sincerely,

Donna F. Doyle

Donna F. Doyle

EUGENE V. MISNER
414 Moreland Road
Ann Arbor, MI 48105

October 22, 1999

Ms. Sarah J. Coburn
Director of Procurement
Glaxo Inc.
Five Moore Drive
Research Triangle Park, NC 27709

Dear Ms. Coburn:

As you are probably aware, the Warner-Lambert Company has recently announced a cutback in the size of its Ann Arbor workforce by some 4,000 employees. My position, unfortunately, was one of many that have been eliminated by the company.

Should you be in the market for a talented, young Procurement Manager for either a corporate or division-level assignment, I would welcome the opportunity to speak with you. A brief summary of my qualifications follows:

- B.S., Chemical Engineering, University of Delaware

- 4 years' corporate procurement experience as follows:
    - 1 year   -   Manager, Engineering Procurement
    - 1 year   -   Senior Buyer, Engineering
    - 1 year   -   Buyer, Specialty Chemicals
    - 1 year   -   Associate Buyer, Packaging Supplies

As you can see, I have had a broad smattering of purchasing experience across a wide range of products (most of a fairly technical nature). My experience includes responsibility for the negotiation and management of multi-million dollar national contracts supplying some 50 Warner-Lambert manufacturing sites. Major contracts that I have handled include those at the $100+ million level.

During my four years with Warner-Lambert, I have been credited with savings in the $10 to $15 million range. These have come about principally as the result of a combination of skillful negotiations and exhaustive research to identify new, more competitive supply sources. Perhaps I could bring similar results to your company.

Should you wish to further explore my background and credentials, please call me at (313) 996-3189. I can be reached between the hours of 8:00 a.m. and 5:30 p.m.

Thank you for your consideration.

Sincerely,

Eugene V. Misner

Eugene V. Misner

ELIZABETH M. PINDER

1901 Roxborough Road, Charlotte, NC 28211

May 2, 1998

Mr. Thomas J. Novack
President
ARCO Chemical Company
3500 West Chester Pike
Newtown Square, PA 19073

Dear Mr. Novack:

I recently read an article in the *Chicago Tribune* about the enormous success of ARCO Chemical Company in the field of specialty chemicals and the major expansion you are planning. I would very much like to be a part of your future plans, and feel I have much to offer a company such as yours as a senior procurement officer.

My qualifications include:

- B.S., Chemistry, Ohio State University

- MBA, Finance, Northwestern University

- 20 years' procurement experience in the chemical industry

  - 2 years - Vice President Procurement, Barlow Chemical Company
  - 2 years - Director of Procurement, Barlow Chemical Company
  - 3 years - Manager Raw Materials Purchasing, Dow Chemical
  - 2 years - Manager Chemicals Purchasing, Dow Chemical
  - 10 years - Various Purchasing Assignments, Dow Chemical

My 20 years of professional and managerial experience as a procurement professional in the chemical industry has prepared me well for a high-growth company such as yours. I am up-to-date on the latest procurement systems and processes and could provide excellent strategic leadership to your procurement function. I have always enjoyed a strong reputation as an innovator who knows how to create and manage a procurement function that returns significant savings to the business.

Perhaps it may be worth your while to meet with me and explore the many ways in which I could save your company time and money. If you agree, I can be reached at (704) 336-2527.

Thank you for your consideration, and I look forward to hearing from you.

Sincerely,

Elizabeth M. Pinder

Elizabeth M. Pinder

RICHARD H. BRADSHAW
5020 Brandin Court
Danbury, CT 06811
(203) 966-1701

February 22, 1999

Mr. Matthew J. Perlman
Director of Technology
Genzyme Corporation
One Kendall Square
Cambridge, MA 02139

Dear Mr. Perlman:

I am a Research Engineer with six years experience in the development of photo imaging products used in the microprocessing field. Currently a key contributor to James River Graphics' research effort in the micrographics field, my key achievements include:

- Lead researcher in the development of JRG's revolutionary new TEP microfilm technology.

- Development of new, non-silver halide film technology for use in consumer photographic market.

- Development of novel, new updatable microfiche for use in microfilm files.

My technical qualifications include:

- Ph.D., Polymer Science, M.I.T., 1993
  M.S., Chemical Engineering, R.P.I., 1991
  B.S., Chemical Engineering, University of Massachusetts, 1989

- Six years R&D product and process development in photo imaging technology.

- Awarded eight U.S. patents on new photo imaging products and technology, with an additional 15 patent disclosures.

I am seeking a position as Group Leader or Research Manger with responsibility for direction of a product development team in the field of photo imaging-related research. Compensation requirements are in the $75,000 to $80,000 range, and I am open to relocation to most areas of the country.

Should my credentials be of interest to Genzyme, I would appreciate hearing from you. I can be reached at my home number most week nights after 7:00 p.m. Thank you for your consideration, and I look forward to hearing from you.

Sincerely,

Richard H. Bradshaw

Richard H. Bradshaw

SANDRA A. WESTON

2408 Orchard Park Drive
Schaumburg, IL 60173

Home: (708) 431-2176
Office: (708) 255-1355

July 23, 1997

Ms. Josephine Bennett
Senior Partner
Pro-Search, Inc.
36 South State Street
Chicago, IL 60606

Dear Ms. Bennett:

Perhaps one of your current clients is in need of a senior account manager for their corporate accounting operations. If so, they may well have an interest in my qualifications:

Educational Qualifications:

- B.A.,   Accounting, University of Wisconsin, 1992
  M.B.A., Finance, Michigan State University, 1994
  C.P.A.,   State of Wisconsin, June 1991

Professional Experience:

- 2 years public accounting experience - Price Waterhouse
- 5 years experience - Kimberly-Clark Corporation as follows:

  1 year   - Assistant Manager, Corporate Accounting
  2 years - Manager, General Ledger Accounting
  1 year   - Accounting Supervisor
  1 year   - Senior Accountant

I am seeking a position as Manager or Director of Corporate Accounting for a major manufacturing company with a direct reporting relationship to the Chief Financial Officer. My compensation requirements are in the $80,000 to $90,000 range, and I am willing to relocate for the right opportunity.

I have an excellent performance record and am considered to be a "high potential" employee by my current employer. Unfortunately, I do not see an opportunity for advancement in the foreseeable future. Outstanding references are readily available upon request.

If I appear to be a match for any of your current search assignments, I would welcome the opportunity to meet with you and will provide you with a complete summary of my qualifications at that time. Thank you for your consideration.

Sincerely,

Sandra A. Weston

Sandra A. Weston

GENE P. BILLINGS
122 East Brunswick Court
Scranton, PA 19226
(717) 539-2406

May 12, 1998

Mr. Anthony C. Burgess
National Sales Manager - Floor Coverings
Armstrong World Industries, Inc.
313 West Liberty Street
Lancaster, PA 17603

Dear Mr. Burgess:

What would you give to be able to hire one of the top sales representatives of your largest competitor? This is your chance!

I am currently the leading Senior Accounts Representative for Burlington Industries' Eastern Region. Major accomplishments include:

- National Sales Award - 1997, 1996, 1995 and 1994
  (top 10% of sales representatives nationally)

- Sales Rep of the Year Award, Eastern Region, 1997
  (First Runner-Up, 1996)

- Increased territory sales volume by 600% in five years

I have been very impressed with your new ceramic tile line as well as other new floor covering lines you have introduced during the last two years. I feel that I could have a major impact on your sales volume if given the opportunity to manage your Eastern Region. With my proven sales ability and your quality products and competitive pricing, I feel certain that I could lead Armstrong to become the number one competitor in the East in less than two years time!

Hopefully, you can see the potential for an excellent marriage here and will give me a call. I would welcome the opportunity to meet with you to discuss the potential for making a significant contribution to your business. Of course, this inquiry is made in the strictest confidence.

Thank you for your consideration and I look forward to the possibility of meeting with you personally.

Sincerely,

Gene P. Billings

Gene P. Billings

MARGO C. BARRINGTON

2246 Gibraltar Drive, Columbus, OH 44392

May 2, 1997

Mr. Daniel P. Corcoran
Director of Marketing
Stouffer Foods Corporation
3003 Bainbridge Road
Solon, OH 44139

Dear Mr. Corcoran:

Could your company use a talented, young Brand Manager who has an excellent record of achieving major increases in sales volume through creative marketing approaches in the consumer products industry? If so, you may want to consider bringing me in for an exploratory interview.

Please consider the following credentials:

- M.B.A., Marketing, Wharton School, 1992

- B.A., Business Administration, Penn State University, 1990

- 5 years marketing experience, Borden Foods, Inc.

    2 years - Senior Brand Manager
    2 years - Brand Manager
    1 year   - Associate Brand Manager

Key accomplishments include:

- Led national marketing roll-out of new fresh pasta line, achieving 60% of market share in less than two years.

- Revitalized sagging yogurt line with change in name and packaging coupled with creative advertising theme (55% increase in sales volume in less than six months).

- Increased market share of powdered drink mix product line by 33 points to become brand market leader in one year.

I am confident that I can make similar contributions to Stouffer Foods, and would welcome the opportunity to meet with you to explore the potential for a profitable career relationship.

Should you have an interest in my credentials, I can be reached at (216) 977-0133 during weeknights.

Thank you for your consideration and I look forward to hearing from you.

Sincerely,

Margo C. Barrington

Margo C. Barrington

ALBERT E. PRENDERGAST
201 N. Athens Way
Lawrenceville, GA 30244
(404) 671-2066

April 23, 1998

Mr. Richard H. Beatty, President
The Bradford Group
Brandywine Corporate Center
Building 5
Malvern, PA 19355

Dear Mr. Beatty:

As an employment agency specializing in the field of Public Affairs, you may wish to be aware of my candidacy. Perhaps one of your client companies is looking for a talented professional with expertise in government and legislative affairs.

I hold a B.S. degree in Political Science from American University and have over five years' experience in the field of governmental and legislative affairs with Southeast National Telephone Company.

In my current position as Manager of Legislative Affairs for the states of Georgia, Florida, Alabama and Tennessee, I am responsible for the management of a staff of three professionals and am accountable for all state legislative matters affecting the business of Southeast National Telephone Company.

Some key accomplishments include:

- Led lobby effort that defeated Bill 334226 requiring a 3% Florida state sales tax surcharge on all local toll phone calls (annual savings $26 million).

- Initiated sponsorship and led successful lobby effort to pass Bill 44.5578A (State of Georgia) allowing Southeast National Telephone to provide long distance services within the state (annual sales revenue potential of $18 to $20 million during next five years).

- Defeated Tennessee House Bill 1996-344A, requiring the replacement of telephone and utility poles every 15 years (annual savings = $9 million).

Should you feel that one of your current search assignments is a suitable match for my qualifications, I would appreciate hearing from you. I can be reached most evenings at my home between the hours of 7:30 and 9:30 p.m.

Thank you for your consideration.

Sincerely,

Albert E. Prendergast

Albert E. Prendergast

JAMES M. McCOY

120 San Gabriel Avenue
Sunnyvale, CA 94086

Home: (401) 296-4779
Office: (408) 739-6700

August 22, 1997

Mr. Samuel H. Pruet
Vice President Manufacturing
Mattel, Inc.
333 Continental Boulevard
El Segundo, CA 90245

Dear Mr. Pruet:

The Mattel Corporation has always enjoyed an excellent reputation as one of the area's outstanding employers, and I have long had an interest in working for your company. Perhaps my dream has the potential to become reality!

I understand that Tom Hardy, Operations Manager at your Pleasantville Plant, has just announced his retirement and that you are about to begin a search for his replacement. Perhaps I could save you the time! Please consider my qualifications for this position:

- M.B.A., Finance, University of Connecticut, 1986
  B.S., Mechanical Engineering, R.P.I., 1984

- Currently Plant Manager for Milton Bradley's Los Angeles Plant, a 350-employee toy manufacturing facility.

- Previously spent four years as Operations Manager for same facility.

- Fully versed in modern manufacturing concepts and approaches including JIT, MRP, high performance work systems, total quality, etc.

Since assuming the position of Plant Manager at Milton Bradley one year ago, I have brought significant improvements as follow:

- Reduced operating costs by 23% ($4 million annual savings)

- Successfully thwarted major union organizing attempt

- Led quality initiative with resultant 68% reduction in consumer complaints

I am confident I could make similar contributions to Mattel, and would welcome the opportunity to meet with you personally to explore this possibility.

Thank you and I look forward to hearing from you shortly.

Sincerely,

James M. McCoy

James M. McCoy

GAIL F. JORDAN
45 Goodwin Drive
Cherry Hill, NJ 08003
Home: (609) 223-4506

April 15, 1999

Mr. James L. Spangler
President
Spangler & Associates, Inc.
6000 Madison Avenue, Ste. 450
New York, NY 10011

Dear Mr. Spangler:

Some recent changes here at Sterling Winthrop have prompted my decision to make a career change. I am therefore sending this brief synopsis of my qualifications to your attention in the event one of your clients may be in search of someone with my credentials.

Highlights of my qualifications are as follow:

- Ph.D., Industrial Psychology, University of Texas

- 18 years human resources experience in the consumer products (The Gillette Company) and pharmaceutical (Sterling Winthrop) industries

As Director of Human Resources for the Corporate Staff of Sterling Winthrop, I currently report to the Senior Vice President of Human Resources and provide a full range of human resources support services to the corporate offices (1,800 employees) of this $7 billion pharmaceutical manufacturer. In this capacity, I direct a staff of 36 employees with functional responsibility for human resources planning, staffing, organization design and development, training, compensation and benefits, and equal opportunity.

I am seeking a senior level human resources management position, preferably at the vice president level, with broad executive leadership responsibility for management of an organization's human resources. Although clearly secondary to job challenge and interest, my compensation requirements (base salary plus bonus) are in the low $100K range.

If this synopsis is of interest, I would be pleased to provide you with a more specific accounting of my qualifications during a face-to-face meeting. Should you wish, I can be reached at my office (Phone: 215-699-0717). Thank you.

Sincerely,

Gail F. Jordan

Gail F. Jordan

LINDA S. McDONALD

5722 Timber Trail, Compton, CA 90510

May 16, 1998

Mr. Michael J. Albertson
Director of Human Resources
Toyota Motor Corporation, USA
19001 S. Western Avenue
Torrance, CA 90509

Dear Mr. Albertson:

I am an experienced employment professional with solid training and experience in recruitment and employment for a Fortune 200 organization. Please take a brief moment to consider my qualifications as follow:

·   MBA, Human Resources Management, Michigan State University.

·   BA, Business Administration, University of Wisconsin.

·   Five years' corporate employment experience with The Alpha Corporation as follows:

   · 2 years = Manager of Technical Employment
   · 2 years = Assistant Manager, Administrative Employment
   · 1 year = College Relations Specialist

My employment experience is broad, covering a wide range of business functions including: marketing and sales, manufacturing, engineering, research, accounting and finance, human resources, public affairs, management information services, law and logistics. Additionally, I have handled all levels of recruitment from entry level professional through vice president.

I am seeking a senior level management position in employment at the corporate level. Ideally, this would be either Director or Manager of Corporate Employment. Should you have an appropriate opening on your corporate employment staff, I would appreciate the opportunity to meet with you. My office phone number is (310) 329-0900. Should you wish to reach me in the evening, my home phone is (310) 451-2910.

I look forward to the possibility of talking with you. Thank you for your consideration.

Sincerely,

Linda S. McDonald

Linda S. McDonald

7

Thank-You Letters

The previous chapters have covered the five types of cover letters. They are the *necessary* letters that should accompany your resume. This chapter describes a letter you don't have to write but will never forget to send if you want a prospective employer to remember your application and regard it favorably. This final letter, sent after being given an interview or receiving a written reply, is a thank-you letter.

This type of letter is sometimes known as a letter of appreciation or simply an appreciation letter. It plays an important role in the employment process. Too often, job seekers overlook basic courtesy in the swirl of activity that accompanies the job-hunting process. Yet, the favorable impression created by a well-written thank-you letter can speak volumes about the manners and character of the employment candidate.

When I was Manager of Technical Employment at Scott Paper Company's corporate offices in Philadelphia, and later, while serving as vice president of a major international executive search firm, I was surprised by the large number of employment candidates who, after being given the opportunity to interview for a position, never thought to send a thank-you to either the search firm or the employer. I would estimate that less than 10 percent of the interviewees took the time to express their appreciation in letter form. This is a discouraging statistic— and a missed opportunity overlooked by the majority of job seekers.

The time, effort, and expense that organizations commit to preparing for and hosting an employment candidate during an interview day deserve a thank-you from the candidate. An administrative assistant must coordinate the visit, finalize and confirm the interview schedule, publish and distribute the schedule and copies of the visitor's resume, arrange for travel, lodging, and so on. Valuable time is also taken from busy work schedules by the various staff members who will participate in the interviewing process. Fairly extensive effort goes into making the stay pleasant and informative. The least that is warranted, under these circumstances, is a brief letter acknowledging this effort and expressing appreciation for the host's hospitality. Don't overlook this basic courtesy if you are interested in making a favorable impression and enhancing interest in your employment candidacy.

It is important to realize that besides the favorable impression created by such letters from the "good manners" standpoint, the thank-you letter offers an additional opportunity to market yourself for the position. Although this is not the principal reason for writing a letter of appreciation, it is an added feature that should not be ignored by the conscientious job seeker. A well-constructed thank-you letter can go a long way not only in communicating the level of your interest in the position, but also in reinforcing the message concerning your unique qualifications that you delivered during the interview. The letter gives you another opportunity to stress your potential value to the hiring organization. A thank-you letter can be the deciding factor in a company's decision to make an employment offer.

ELEMENTS OF EFFECTIVE THANK-YOU LETTER

Review of the samples contained in this chapter will reveal the elements required to make thank-you letters particularly effective. These are:

1. Greeting or salutation.
2. Expression of appreciation for interview.
3. Statement of interest in position.
4. Value statement.
5. Restatement of appreciation for interview.
6. Close.

Normally, these elements are incorporated into the letter's construction in the order in which they appear here. The following letters will illustrate some variations in how these important elements may be used to your advantage.

September 23, 1997

Ms. Martha T. Randolph
Director of Human Resources
Astar Corporation
1200 Commerce Drive
Atlanta, GA 16385

Dear Martha:

I wanted to let you know how much I enjoyed my recent trip to Astar Corporation and the opportunity to interview for the position of Engineering Manager. The day was certainly an enjoyable and informative one, and I appreciated the chance to meet with you and the other members of the interview team who all did such an excellent job of helping me to understand both the requirements of the position and Astar's work environment.

The position as Engineering Manager of your Air Products Division sounds like a challenging and exciting opportunity, and I wanted to reiterate my strong interest in this position.

In my discussions with Tony, he mentioned that besides the normal responsibilities of a Division Engineering Manager, the primary thrust of this position over the next two to three years will be the technology transfer of six new products which are critical components of the Company's business strategy. This is an area, of course, where I have had significant experience, and I know that I could be of real help to Astar in successfully bringing these products to market. Additionally, I feel I could provide meaningful assistance with your efforts to implement a corporate-wide TQM program, since I was a key member of the corporate steering committee instrumental in implementing a highly successful TQM program here at Winston Company.

Again, Martha, I appreciated the opportunity to visit Astar Corporation. Please pass along my sincere "thanks" to the other members of the interview team who helped to make the day so enjoyable.

I look forward to hearing from you shortly.

Sincerely,

Thomas R. Reardon

Thomas R. Reardon

June 16, 1996

Mr. Walter F. Baxter
Senior Vice President
The Richfield Company
Executive Search Consultants
4520 Park Avenue, Suite 1400
New York, NY 18773-1982

Dear Walter:

I wish to thank you for your time and hospitality during my visit to New York City this past Thursday. I appreciated your patience and thoroughness in helping me to understand the needs of your client for the position of Director of Marketing.

Although, at this stage of the process, I know it is customary for search consultants to maintain the confidentiality of their client, I did want to let you know of my preliminary interest in the position we discussed. It would appear to be an excellent match for my background and qualifications, and certainly is "on target" with respect to my current career objectives.

My strengths in competitive intelligence should be of real interest to your client in their desire to establish a competitive intelligence function as a key component of corporate marketing strategy. Additionally, my track record in the successful launch of several major consumer products (most of which have achieved either # 1 or # 2 in market share), should also prove appealing to your client.

Based upon our discussion, my interest in this position is quite strong and I would welcome the opportunity to proceed to the next step. I would hope to hear from you shortly.

Again, Walter, thank you for your hospitality.

Sincerely,

Barbara A. Swanson

Barbara A. Swanson

March 25, 1997

Ms. Linda R. Shilling
Manager of College Recruiting
The Waverly Company, Inc.
34 Industry Blvd.
Milwaukee, WI 94597

Dear Ms. Shilling:

I returned to the University of Wisconsin, after yesterday's interviews at The Waverly Company, thinking how exciting it will be to finally launch my career in Engineering and put my last four years of academic training to practical use. My visit with you and the other members of the interview team did much to heighten my level of excitement and anticipation. What an exciting opportunity!

I wanted to let you know how much I appreciated the chance to interview with Waverly. I am most appreciative of the efforts of both you and the other team members in making my day a very enjoyable and informative one. The position of Project Engineer, as described during my visit, sounds just like the kind of challenge that I am seeking at this early stage of my career.

Ms. Shilling, my strong academic achievement and interest in fluid mechanics would appear to be an excellent match for your needs. Although my interests are diverse, fluid mechanics has always been a subject of particular interest to me. My propensity for creativity, as supported by my background as an amateur artist, should also prove helpful. I look forward to working with Dr. Johnson on development of the new airlay process, and the challenge of developing an entirely new, revolutionary way of manufacturing paper webs.

Please pass along my "thanks" to the other members of the interview team for their time and effort in providing me with an exciting and interesting visit. I appreciated their thoroughness and patience in answering my many questions.

I look forward to hearing from you in the near future, and hope your decision on my employment candidacy will be a positive one.

Thanks again for your hospitality.

Sincerely,

Mary A. Livingston

Mary A. Livingston

April 21, 1998

Mr. Edward C. Cox
Manager of Corporate Accounting
Wilson Enterprises, Inc.
1525 Executive Row
Claymore Business Park
Wilmington, DE 19898

Dear Ed:

Thanks for the opportunity to visit with you this past Wednesday to discuss the position of Senior Tax Accountant on your staff. I certainly appreciated your hospitality.

Since it seems to capture so many of my particular technical strengths and specific interests, the position of Senior Tax Accountant, as described during my visit, is of great interest to me and I would welcome the chance to further explore this opportunity with your organization.

Reflecting back on our conversation, it would appear that I have most of the key qualifications you seek. In particular, my intimate knowledge of the tax aspects of the Alpha General Ledger System should prove additive to your efforts to painlessly launch this new general ledger system in February of next year. My background in international tax, especially in Europe, should also prove quite beneficial to Wilson's plans to start new ventures in both Germany and the U.K. next year. I can certainly help you to avoid some of the major and costly pitfalls from the tax standpoint.

All in all, I feel that I have the necessary background and skills to be quite successful in the position of Senior Tax Accountant, and would hope that you view my candidacy favorably. I am certain that I can make a real contribution to your organization.

Thanks again, Ed, and I look forward to hearing from you shortly.

Sincerely,

David D. Carter

January 14, 1997

Mr. Richard D. Walker
Director of Marketing
Lorton Company, Inc.
20 Industrial Court
Waymar Industrial Park
Denver, CO 16284

Dear Dick:

I wanted to thank you for the opportunity to visit Lorton Company on Wednesday of this week to explore the position of Associate Brand Manager for your new soft drink beverage, Quench. I certainly appreciated the hospitality of both you and the members of your staff, and the thorough way in which my interview was handled. The day was quite informative and enjoyable!

By comparison with most of the opportunities I am currently considering, the position of Associate Brand Manager - Quench sounds intriguing, and my interest in this position is quite high. In particular, the chance to develop the complete marketing strategy for a new product, for a fresh MBA graduate, is exciting and is exactly the kind of opportunity for which I am looking.

As you are aware, I am graduating near the top of my class at Wharton Business School with a heavy course emphasis in marketing. My interest in consumer products marketing is especially strong. These qualifications. coupled with my prior marketing experience with the Kraft Foods Company, will hopefully make me a particularly attractive candidate to the Lorton Company. I feel I have both the training and motivation required for success in the consumer marketing field, and that I have the potential to make substantive contributions to my new employer.

Thanks again for your hospitality during my visit, and please pass along my special "thanks" to the balance of the interview team for their part in making my visit a very pleasant and informative one.

I look forward to hearing from you, and the possibility of further exploring career opportunities with the Lorton Company. Thank you.

Sincerely,

Willa B. Brookes

Willa B. Brookes

Index